WORLD RELIGIONS

AFRICAN TRADITIONAL RELIGION

THIRD EDITION

WORLD RELIGIONS

African Traditional Religion
Baha'i Faith
Buddhism
Catholicism & Orthodox Christianity
Confucianism
Daoism
Hinduism
Islam
Judaism
Native American Religions
Protestantism
Shinto
Sikhism
Zoroastrianism

WORLD RELIGIONS

AFRICAN TRADITIONAL RELIGION

THIRD EDITION

by
Aloysius M. Lugira
Series Editors: Joanne O'Brien and Martin Palmer

CHELSEA HOUSE
PUBLISHERS
An imprint of Infobase Publishing

African Traditional Religion, Third Edition

Chelsea House
An imprint of Infobase Publishing
132 West 31st Street
New York NY 10001

Library of Congress Cataloging-in-Publication Data
Lugira, Aloysius Muzzanganda.
  African traditional religion / by Aloysius M. Lugira. —3rd ed.
      p. cm. — (World religions)
  Includes bibliographical references and index.
  ISBN 978-1-60413-103-1
  1. Africa—Religion. 2. Africa—Religious life and customs. I.
Title. II. Series.

  BL2400.L84 2009
  299.6—dc22

          2008051188

This book was produced for Chelsea House by Bender Richardson White, Uxbridge, U.K.
Project Editor: Lionel Bender
Text Editor: Ronne Randall
Designer: Ben White
Picture Researchers: Joanne O'Brien and Kim Richardson
Maps and symbols: Stefan Chabluk
Composition by Bender Richardson White, United Kingdom
Cover printed by Creative Printing
Book printed and bound by Creative Printing
Date printed: March, 2010

Printed in China

10 9 8 7 6 5 4 3 2

This book is printed on acid-free paper.

CONTENTS

PREFACE

Almost from the start of civilization, more than 10,000 years ago, religion has shaped human history. Today more than half the world's population practice a major religion or indigenous spiritual tradition. In many 21st-century societies, including the United States, religion still shapes people's lives and plays a key role in politics and culture. And in societies throughout the world increasing ethnic and cultural diversity has led to a variety of religions being practiced side by side. This makes it vital that we understand as much as we can about the world's religions.

The World Religions series, of which this book is a part, sets out to achieve this aim. It is written and designed to appeal to both students and general readers. The books offer clear, accessible overviews of the major religious traditions and institutions of our time. Each volume in the series describes where a particular religion is practiced, its origins and history, its central beliefs and important rituals, and its contributions to world civilization. Carefully chosen photographs complement the text, and sidebars, a map, fact file, glossary, bibliography, and index are included to help readers gain a more complete understanding of the subject at hand.

These books will help clarify what religion is all about and reveal both the similarities and differences in the great spiritual traditions practiced around the world today.

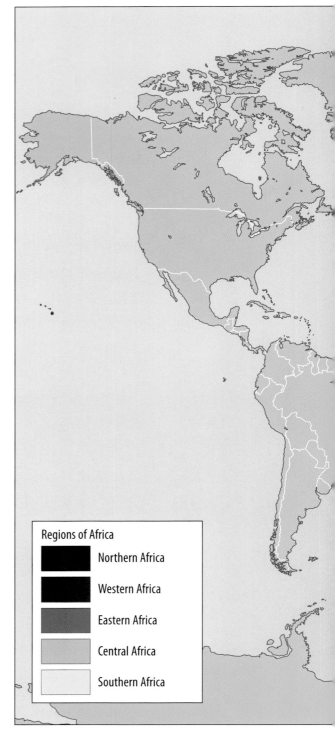

Regions of Africa

Northern Africa

Western Africa

Eastern Africa

Central Africa

Southern Africa

AFRICAN TRADITIONAL RELIGION

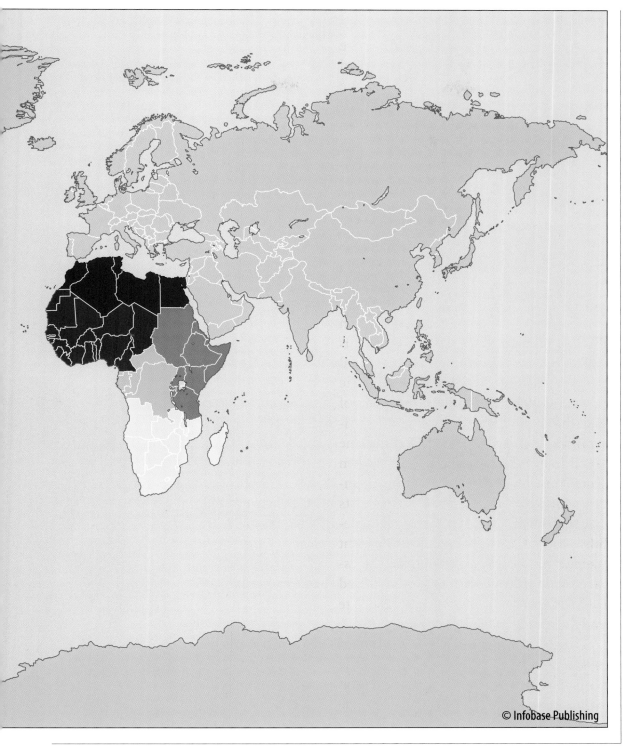

CHAPTER 1

INTRODUCTION: AFRICA AND ITS PEOPLE

Iwa ni csin
"Character is religion."

This proverb of the Yoruba people of Nigeria, West Africa, expresses a fundamental truth about the character of the African people. When they are in need they turn to superhuman powers for help. They address their prayers to a God, either directly or indirectly, through lesser gods or spiritual go-betweens.

When they address their God the elders of the Kikuyu people of Kenya, for example, gather the people of the community together under a sacred tree. A procession arrives. At its head are two children. A boy carries a calabash, or gourd, filled with milk; a girl carries a calabash of honey-beer. A lamb follows them, and last come the elders. When the procession reaches the base of the sacred tree, the leading elder takes the calabashes from the children. Facing Mount Kenya, he raises the calabashes and addresses God with the following prayer.

Acacia trees growing on the savanna of Tanzania. The extensive spirit world of African religion includes spirit guardians that reside in natural landmarks such as rivers, mountains, or trees. These places often become the focus of communal ritual.

"Reverend Elder who lives on Kere-Nyaga ('Mountain of Brightness,' which is the Kikuyu name for Mount Kenya). You who make mountains tremble and rivers flood; we offer you this sacrifice that you may bring us rain. People and children are crying; sheep, goats, and cattle are crying. Mwene-Nyaga ('Possessor of Brightness,' the Kikuyu name for God), we beseech you, with the blood of this lamb, which we are going to sacrifice to you. Refined honey and milk we have brought for you. We praise you in the same way as our forefathers used to praise you under this very same tree, and you heard them and brought them rain. We beseech you to accept this, our sacrifice, and bring us rain of prosperity." The people respond, "Peace, we beseech you, Ngai, peace be with us."

More than 930 million people live on the African continent. Many are at home in the bustling cities of the north—Cairo, Tripoli, Tunis, Algiers—where the religion today is predominantly Islam. In sub-Saharan Africa, especially in the eastern and western coastal countries and in southern Africa, Christianity is the predominant religion. However throughout Africa, especially in central Saharan regions, many people live in communities that at least to some extent follow traditional ways of life that stretch back thousands of years.

Beginning in prehistoric times the people of Africa gathered in groups related by family ties and similar needs. These communities developed their own individual languages, cultures, practices, and religions. Although waves of exploration and modernization have had their impact on the traditional African way of life, it is estimated that there are more than 6,000 different peoples in Africa today. Many of these people continue to live by the spiritual influence of their ancestral way of life. Even after they have left their native vil-

FOLLOWERS OF AFRICAN RELIGION

African countries where African religion is practiced by more than 33 percent of the population

Benin 51.5%
Sierra Leone 46.4%
Guinea-Bissau 45.4%
Botswana 38.8%
Mozambique 35.1%
Liberia 34.1%
Ivory Coast 33.5%
Burkina Faso 33.5%
(Source: www.adherents.com)

AFRICAN RELIGION AS MANIFESTED BY AFRICAN ETHNICITIES

Northern Africa Obsolete Religions:
Berber religion
Cushite religion
Egyptian religion

Eastern Africa Obsolete Religion:
Aksumite religion

Eastern Africa Living Religions:
Dinka religion
Nuer religion
Shilluk religion
Galla religion
Acholi religion
Ateso religion
Baganda religion
Bagisu religion
Banyankore religion
Langi religion
Banyoro religion
Lugbara religion
Akamba religion
Akikuyu religion
Maasai religion
Bahaya religion
Bachagga religion
Bafipa religion
Bahehe religion
Bamakonda religion
Banyakyusa Religion
Basukuma religion
Banyamwezi religion

Central Africa Living Religions:
Babemba religion
Bacongo religion

Baluba religion
Bandembu religion
Banyakyusa religion
Baka religion
Bambuti religion
Shona religion
Banyarwanda religion
Barundi religion

Southern Africa Living Religions:
!Kung Religion
Khoi religion
Lovedu religion
San religion
Sotho religion
Swazi religion
Tswana religion
Xhosa religion
Zulu religion

Western Africa Living Religions:
Ashanti religion
Bambara religion
Dogon religion
Edo religion
Ewe religion
Fang religion
Fanti religion
Fon religion
Ga religion
Igbo religion
Mende religion
Nupe religion
Tiv religion
Yoruba religion

lages to live in the cities, most Africans still identify themselves according to the heritage of their ancestors.

A POPULATION OF BELIEVERS

African religion remains very much alive. Even those countries on the West African coast that have had a Christian presence since the 15th century still have high percentages of adherents of African religion. In five of these countries—Benin, Mozambique, Guinea-Bissau, Liberia, and the Ivory Coast—African religion is the majority religion. In Sierra Leone, Botswana, and Burkina Faso more than 33 percent follow African religion, although it is not the religion of the majority. These figures represent people who primarily follow African traditional religion; however, there are also Christians and Muslims who still practice elements of traditional African religion alongside their professed beliefs. This accounts for the varying figures that are sometimes seen in

An Adinkira symbol dyed on a cloth. The Ashanti people of Ghana in West Africa have developed a variety of Adinkira, designs that have symbolic meaning. These designs are often stamped on cloth known as Adinkira cloth and used for decoration. The Adinkira, right, is the Gye Nyame, which means "Except God (I fear none)." It expresses the supremacy of God.

numbers of adherents of African religion. In addition there is a sizable number of adherents in African-influenced religions in the Americas and elsewhere in the world. If numbers of adherents are indicative of the continued existence of a religion, then the numbers of adherents of African religion ensure its continuation in the future.

For many people, combining traditional religion with either Christianity or Islam is also a way of life. In particular, what is known variously as indigenous Christianity or independent churches have arisen throughout sub-Saharan Africa and probably represent the largest current manifestation of traditional African religion, albeit in a pluralist context.

THE AFRICAN CONTINENT

To understand African religion, it helps to look at Africa itself. Africa is the second largest continent on Earth. Only Asia is larger. Africa's 11.7 million square miles make it about three times the size of Europe and twice the size of the United States, including Alaska. On the north, where it shares the waters of the Mediterranean Sea with Spain, Italy, and Greece, it lies close to Europe. Only the narrow Red Sea separates it from the Middle East. Its western shore stretches along the North and South Atlantic Ocean, and its eastern shore the entire length of the Indian Ocean.

Because of its vast size Africa is a land of contrasts. It contains one of the world's greatest deserts, the Sahara, which stretches across the north-central part of the continent, dividing north from south. North of the Sahara lie countries rich with ancient tradition. Ancient Egypt, whose pharaoh once ruled vast holdings in the Middle East, was one of the most powerful countries in the world. Carthage, a great city-state centuries before the Roman Empire, lay in what is now Tunisia. Trading with Greece and Rome, and with Asia to the east, the North Africans developed cosmopolitan cultures. They built large cities, erected monuments, and developed written language. They worshipped their own ancient gods. Later their traditional religions would be swept aside by first Christianity and then Islam.

A member of the Tuareg community, who live mostly in the Saharan and Sahelian regions of Africa. The Tuareg are seminomadic and travel with their herds on a seasonal basis. *Tuareg* means "people of the veil"— Tuareg men have traditionally worn a veil across their faces. The Tuareg are Muslim, but their traditional rituals and beliefs, including widespread beliefs in a spirit world, overlap with those of Islam.

THE SUB-SAHARA

Below the Sahara is a land of enormous variety, from snow-covered mountains and deep valleys with great rivers to open grasslands to rainforest. Cut off from known civilization by the huge, empty Sahara, these lands remained largely untouched by outside exploration for centuries. However they were not uninhabited. Indeed humanity as we know it may have sprung from deep within the African continent. Recent scientific studies in Kenya and elsewhere in Africa strongly suggest that Africa may be the birthplace of the human race.

AFRICAN PEOPLES AND THEIR RELIGIONS

Over many centuries the African peoples below the Sahara lived in close relationship with the land. Some were nomads—wanderers—who followed the animals they hunted or established camps where their herds could graze. Others farmed or lived off the land, gathering native plants for food. Often they were widely separated from their closest neighbors. Living more or less in isolation, they developed their own languages and customs. They also developed religious practices that served their particular lives and needs.

African religion is not the only religion found in Africa today. However, it is the only religion that can claim to have originated in Africa. Other religions found in Africa have their origins in other parts of the world.

AFRICAN RELIGION AND OTHER RELIGIONS

African religion differs from religions such as Judaism, Christianity, and Islam in a number of ways. Although individual peoples may remember legendary figures from their history, African religion has no single founder or central historical figure. Like Native American religions and Asian

Physical and Spiritual Suffering

African religion teaches that people are made up of moral, social, spiritual, and physical parts. These parts function together. If any part is out of balance, the person may become physically ill or suffer spiritually. That is why a conflict with another person may make someone sick, or a moral misdeed may bring about misfortune.

COMMON THEMES IN AFRICAN LIFE

Although traditional African religion varies widely from region to region and people to people, there are a number of things that they all have in common.

- All things in the universe are part of a whole. There is no sharp distinction between the sacred and the nonsacred.
- In most African traditions there is a Supreme Being: a creator, sustainer, provider, and controller of all creation.
- Serving with the Creator are a variety of lesser and intermediary gods and guardian spirits. These lesser gods are constantly involved in human affairs. People communicate with these gods through rituals, sacrifices, and prayers.
- The human condition is imperfect and always will be. Sickness, suffering, and death are all fundamental parts of life. Suffering is caused by sins and misdeeds that offend the gods and ancestors, or by being out of harmony with society.
- Ritual actions may relieve the problems and sufferings of human life, either by satisfying the offended gods or by resolving social conflicts. Rituals help to restore people to the traditional values and renew their commitment to a spiritual life.
- Human society is communal. Ancestors, the living, the living-dead, and those yet to be born are all an important part of the community. The relationships between the worldly and the otherworldly help to guide and balance the lives of the community. Humans need to interact with the spirit world, which is all around them.

religions such as Shinto and Daoism, it originates with the people themselves. It is an expression of many thousands of years of living close to the land and of seeking answers to the mysteries of life: Why are we here? How do we live well? Why do we die? African religion has no churches or mosques like those of Christianity or Islam. Instead it has shrines constructed according to the traditions of the particular geographical area. People may also turn to a geographical or natural feature, such as a mountain or a large tree, as a focus for worship.

In African religion there is no single ordained priesthood. Religious duties are carried out by a variety of religious leaders. There are priests and priestesses, healers, diviners, mediums, seers, rainmakers, elders, and rulers, each with a special role in maintaining the spiritual life of the community and its people.

THE ORAL TRADITION

Traditional African lore has always been passed down orally. There is no written set of beliefs, no "holy book" such as the Bible or the Quran. Cultural beliefs and rules for living are passed down from generation to generation by word of mouth. Most African peoples have no written language, but members of the community are trained from childhood to perform prodigious acts of memorization, reciting the whole history of the community for successive generations.

An African father and child in their village. Community values are a central force in African life and the African view of the world is focused on being part of a communal group.

BASIC BELIEFS

Followers of African religion make no distinction between religion and other aspects of their lives. Their beliefs are so closely bound to their culture that religion and culture are one. Religion is therefore not something people do at certain times and in certain places, but it is part of the fabric of living. Although a Supreme Being is above the living, lesser gods, spirits, and ancestors walk beside the living and guide them in the direction they must go. They are sometimes displeased by those who do not heed them. People and gods are constantly interacting through ritual, prayer, and sacrifice, but mostly through the business of living.

Among African peoples community, culture, and religion are tightly bound together. The African view of the world is fundamentally one of being part of a communal group. People believe in sharing their property and services, and they expect the other members of the community to share with them. According to noted scholar John Mbiti they believe that "whatever happens to the individual happens to the whole group, and whatever happens to the group happens to the individual. The individual can only say, 'I am, because we are, and since we are, therefore I am.'" In this community spirit lies their security. (In John Mbiti, *African Religions & Philosophy*.)

AFRICA AND ITS HISTORY

Although much of Africa was isolated from the rest of the world, the areas along the coasts developed important cultures. By 3400 B.C.E. Egypt was a flourishing empire with a highly developed religion. The pyramids are its most visible and lasting testimony. However although they represent a triumph of technology, Egyptian pyramids are more than just great wonders of the world. They are also religious structures. Spiritually pyramids are ritual objects that reflect the ancient connection of kingship to African religion, along with belief in life hereafter and immortality.

Egyptian religion was not the only religion in ancient Africa. Judaism originated in the Middle East, but as early as 1300 B.C.E. groups of Hebrew peoples were living on the African continent, primarily in Egypt. Since biblical times in Ethiopia, there have lived thousands of African Jews, known to Ethiopians as Falashas. These so-called Black Jews of Ethiopia practice a religion based entirely on the Old Testament of the Bible but including certain Ethiopian Afri-

The Pyramid of Cheops and the Sphinx at Giza, outside Cairo, Egypt. The pyramids were the burial places of the pharaohs, the kings of Egypt, in the period known as the Old Kingdom (2649 B.C.E.–2150 B.C.E.). The word for pyramid in ancient Egyptian was *mr,* meaning "place of ascension," because it enabled the pharaoh to join the Sun god, Re.

can religious elements. Like other Ethiopians they believe in and use amulets, charms, and magic ritual and prayers.

EARLY CHRISTIANITY IN AFRICA

According to Christian tradition Mary and Joseph, the parents of Jesus Christ, fled to Egypt with the baby Jesus to escape persecution. So in one sense Christianity came to Africa even before its founding. Some of the earliest Christian communities were in North Africa. When Christianity began its spread out of the Middle East it moved into Greece, and from there to Greek colonies. Historians believe that Christianity first came into Africa around 40 C.E. through Alexandria, a city of the Hellenic Empire founded by Alexander the Great. At about the same time a Christian community arose in Egypt that was made up of native Egyptians. The Copts, a Christian tradition, trace their origins to the preaching of Saint Mark, one of the writers of the Christian Gospels, who visited Egypt.

A second way in which Christianity spread to Africans was through Carthage, a Roman province that lay in what is now Tunisia. From about 44 B.C.E. Carthage was culturally Roman; its official language was Latin. The official religion was worship of the Roman gods. Christians were persecuted and even killed. Persecution seems to have worked against the Romans, however, because Christianity grew rapidly in North Africa. African Christianity produced such great leaders as Tertullian,

The Church of Saint George in Lalibela, in the Amhara region of Ethiopia. This rock-hewn church, built in the 13th century, is an important pilgrimage site for members of the Ethiopian Orthodox Church.

Saint Augustine, Saint Cyprian, and Saints Perpetua and Felicity. At least one writer, Tertullian, recognized the importance of the African religious concepts of God to developing Christianity.

In 350 C.E. the ancient kingdom of Aksum, known as Ethiopia today, officially embraced Christianity. At that time the Aksumite king Ezana, originally a strong adherent of his African religion, converted to Christianity. Aksumite Christianity, later called Ethiopian Christianity, has its roots in the Coptic Christianity of Egypt.

AFRICAN RELIGION AND ISLAM

Islam means "submission to the will of God." The creed of Islam is "There is no god but Allah [God], and Muhammad is His prophet." When Muslims arrived in Africa in the seventh century C.E. they did not identify African religion as a religion. They called the native people *kaffirs,* which means "infidels"— people who have no faith, or unbelievers. The name stuck, and Africans came to be known as people with no faith.

The early Muslims did not wage a holy war against African religion or practice forced conversions. However, Islam proved to be an attractive religion to many Africans, particularly in the north, who may have found similarities between their religion and Islam. Today Islam is one of the most dynamic religions in Africa. It is well represented in practically all African nations. In some African countries such as Libya and Morocco it is the predominant religion.

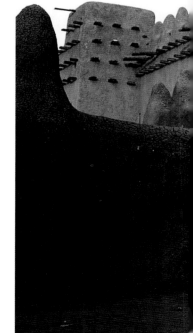

THE ARRIVAL OF THE PORTUGUESE

The Portuguese came to Africa during the 15th century. Prince Henry the Navigator hoped to find a safe new access to Asia and Africa and their treasures, which included pepper, spices, gold, ivory, and precious gems. He received the blessing of the pope, who authorized Portugal and Spain to conquer and possess lands and their riches as well as to pass on the message of Christianity.

There has been a mosque on this site in Djenné in Mali since the 13th century. The current mosque was built of clay by traditional methods between 1906 and 1909.

CULTURAL MISUNDERSTANDINGS

The expeditions usually included chaplains and priests. Sailing along the West and East African coasts, they preached the Christian message to the people they met and took advantage of African hospitality. Eventually they established African Christian communities. However they were to be disappointed. African peoples had welcomed them warmly. But that did not mean that they were ready to give up their cultures and beliefs. The missionaries failed to appreciate the African religion and culture on which the welcome was based, and misunderstanding arose. In frustration the missionaries developed hostile attitudes toward the people. Finally they succumbed to the temptations of the slave trade. Portuguese-sponsored Christianity in Africa ended badly.

EUROPEAN MISSIONARY ACTIVITY

During the 19th century European countries staked claims to African lands in the rush to build empires. This so-called scramble for Africa saw African countries divided among the British, the French, the Germans, and the Dutch, among others. Overwhelmingly Christian, they invited a new wave of Christian missionaries, who came bringing "missions Christianity" with them. Missionaries to Africa included not only Roman Catholic priests, as in the case of the Portuguese and Spanish, but also clerics and laypeople of various Protestant denominations.

UNDERSTANDING AFRICAN CULTURE

The missionaries established schools and hospitals and began preaching the Gospel of Christianity. They were well-meaning, but they had little understanding of the cultures they were entering. Their intent was to bring Christianity to a continent they believed to have no true religion. They meant to stamp out African religious practices they saw as superstition and ignorance.

Living and working among the African people, some members of missionary societies began to appreciate Africans and African religion. They began to make the effort to understand the culture. From this effort they could finally begin to establish a Christian relationship with African religion. Christianity is now the majority religion within Africa followed by more than 46 percent of the continent's population.

UNITY AND DIVERSITY IN AFRICAN RELIGIONS

Although it is possible to make some generalizations about African religion, it is important to remember that African religions are not one, but many. African religions have a great variety of rituals, myths, beliefs, and deities. Yet in spite of their differences from each other and from many other world religions, they share with each other and with most other faiths the goal of guiding individuals safely through the passages of life, from birth and puberty, marriage and maturity, to death and ancestorhood. They mark not only the seasons of life, each with its particular responsibilities and duties, but also the seasons of the year and the cycles of time. They answer the questions of why there is suffering and death in the world and offer ways of dealing with human pain. Finally they provide a way for the people who follow them to be in touch with the spiritual in themselves and in the universe.

There are as many African religions as there are African peoples. However in their diversity they are one. Whether African religion is based in Central Africa, eastern Africa, western Africa, or southern Africa, the belief in a Supreme Being, superhuman beings, and honoring ancestors are its cornerstones. They point to the same understanding.

CHAPTER 2

THE BEGINNING OF TIME: THE ORAL TRADITION

African peoples have wonderful tales to tell about the beginning of time. Traditionally the elders of the village gather the children and tell them about times when the world was young, when animals could talk, when heroes walked among humankind, when their God made the Earth and everything in it. In the hands of the skilled storyteller the characters come alive, and the children will never forget them. The stories are entertaining, but entertainment is not their primary goal. As they listen, the children are absorbing the myths and the culture of their community.

HOW TRADITION IS PASSED ON

Living close to nature, Africans have always observed the world around them. Looking up, they saw the vast expanse of the sky. Around them they saw oceans, seas, lakes, rivers, forests, animals, and many other marvels of creation. They pondered the kinds of

Masai girls doing beadwork. The Masai are a seminomadic people living in Kenya and northern Tanzania. The Masai have a body of oral law, and major decisions in the community are governed by elders. Their Supreme Being, called Enkai, has a dual nature with benevolent and vengeful sides.

An elderly San (Bushmen) hunter tells a story of magical powers in the Kalahari Desert in Namibia.

AFRICAN TRADITIONAL RELIGION

questions that humankind has asked for untold centuries. How did the world come to be? What hand fashioned us and put us here? What does it mean to be alive?

Over centuries people have formed answers to such questions, often in the form of stories, myths, and proverbs. These answers were passed down by word of mouth from one generation to the next. In this way oral traditions, many of which address questions of existence from the beginning of time, are established. The oral traditions constitute the method of transmitting history and religious traditions by spoken rather than written means. In African traditional communities it was part of home education to memorize those traditions with great accuracy.

Oral traditions are passed on in a variety of forms—in myths, legends, stories, and proverbs. Stories generally say something about life in order to educate and entertain the community. Myths deal with the divine. They have religious subjects, such as the origin of the universe and of nature. They address and answer questions like, Where did humankind come from? How are human beings expected to act as they travel through life? What is the destiny of the human race? Legends are a body of stories about families, people, and particularly heroes of the community. Often based on real people and facts, they have been told and retold until they become part of the lore of the community as a whole. Proverbs are short statements that express wisdom about creation and human experience.

CREATION MYTHS AND THE FALL OF HUMANKIND

From their earliest beginnings, African people have asked questions about their existence. Such questions as, Who are we? How did we come to be here? How should we understand our place in this world? have given rise to the rich and varied creation myths of African peoples.

Myths of creation tell of the sacred beginnings of the people. They usually center on a Supreme Being who, according to African oral tradition, created the world. They recognize the special position the Creator has given to humankind. In the creation myth of the Yoruba people, for example, the Supreme Being, Olodumare, enlists the help of Orisha Nla ("the Great God") to make a world out of "magic earth." Orisha Nla fashions human beings out of earth, but only Olodumare knows the secret of how to give the bodies life. "To this day," the myth ends, "Orisha Nla, through the agency of parents, makes the body, but only the Supreme Being can give it life." (In J. F. Bierlein, *Parallel Myths.*)

African creation myths often tell about the special relationship between a God and the first people, when the heavens were very close to Earth. However humankind, being imperfect, made mistakes for which they must be punished. The Dinka people say that once a rope hung down from heaven for people to climb up when they wanted to talk to their God. But an old woman mashing yams kept hitting the underside of heaven with her pestle and, weary of the noise, the God pulled up the rope and withdrew the heavens to a higher plane. Still, people are always encouraged to make up for their failures. African myths commonly conclude with a lesson about the importance of people living well in this world.

HEROES AND LEGENDS

Human life is generally marked by success and failure as well as a variety of minor ups and downs. Hero tales and legends focus on success, encouraging a positive group image. In African traditions, many heroes are human beings who are deified, that is, elevated to the status of gods. Through their acts on Earth they become associates of the Supreme Being. A hero may be someone who does a great deed for the community or someone who seems touched by the gods, especially chosen from childhood for some higher purpose.

Lubaale Mukasa, a god of the Baganda people of East Africa, is an example of a deified hero, a human who has become a god. (The title Lubaale refers to a spiritual being.) When, as a child, he disappeared from his home and appeared mysteriously on another island, the people there thought he must be superhuman to have appeared, seemingly out of nowhere. He refused to eat

Bushmen or Baswara people setting traps to catch food. The Baswara, who live in the Kalahari Desert in Botswana, are the second-largest group of indigenous hunter-gatherers in Africa. Their traditional life, with beliefs and lifestyle closely tied to the land, is currently changing. They are controversially being encouraged by the government to move outside their traditional reserves to settlements in a government scheme to integrate them into modern life.

Masai warriors in northern Tanzania perform a coming-of-age "jumping dance." The Masai are cattle-herders, and they believe that Enkai (their Supreme Being and rain god) granted all cattle to them for safekeeping when the Earth and sky split.

anything but the heart and liver of an ox, and he drank its blood, confirming the people's opinion that he was a god. The people soon began consulting him on matters of health and money. When he disappeared as mysteriously as he had arrived, Lubaale Mukasa was acknowledged as one of the highest-ranking gods of their people.

STORIES AND FABLES

Stories and fables usually illustrate some truth about human nature and end with a stated or unstated moral. Such stories are partly for entertainment, but they are more than just amusing tales. They are the African way of teaching and passing down ethics, or right behavior, to the next generation. One of the most famous African folk heroes is Ananse, the spider. Ananse is the hero of many folktales of the Akan people of West Africa. The Ananse tales have crossed from West Africa to the Americas, where they are familiar to many children.

Ananse is a trickster. Tricksters may be human or animal or a little of both, but they all have superhuman powers that they can use for good or for harm. They also suffer from many of the character flaws that ordinary humans have, such as greed and envy. As a result, they are often caught in their own snares. Stories about Ananse, or as he is usually called, Father Ananse, attribute great skill and ingenuity to him. In one tale Ananse tries to take back the wisdom he has distributed in the world by storing it in a large pot. However, when he is challenged by his son Ntikuma, Ananse angrily allows the pot to fall from the top of a tree, and human beings are able to gather it up for themselves.

Proverbs in African Society

Proverbs teach reverence for and appreciation of authority; the realization that God the Creator is a supreme being, reverence for justice, human sympathy and fellow feeling among individuals, the ability to [turn away from] bitterness and learn from painful experiences, and the futility of envy and competitiveness. They help you to understand that if you twist the arm of justice, you twist the morals of the society. We cannot all hope to be like the maize (corn). The maize has good luck all the time. It goes to the soil naked and returns with good luck with hundreds of children. Look at your five fingers. Are they equal? So are human beings. The old man is wise because he is in his second childhood and, like a child, he is always ready to learn.

(In Ryszard Pachocinski, *Proverbs of Africa: Human Nature in the Nigerian Oral Tradition.*)

The Nupe people of West Africa express their God's being without end in the proverb "God will outlive eternity." Proverbs are short sayings that express a recognized truth. Because people repeat them often, they are easy to remember. African people

A bronze mask of a leopard. The leopard, like the lion, symbolizes ritual power. The leopard is also a symbol of royalty—for example, the leopard represents the spiritual aspect of the kingdom of Benin in Nigeria.

The Shining One

The Akan people of West Africa have many proverbs that are related to their creation myths. Their name for God is Nyame, which means "the Supreme Being," "the Shining One," "the Originator," and "first mover of everything." Here are some of the ways in which their proverbs depict him:

No one points out the Nyame to a child.

The Earth is wide, but Nyame is chief.

All people are Nyame's offspring; no one is the offspring of Earth.

Says Hawk: All Nyame did is good.

The order Nyame has settled, living people cannot subvert.

There is no by-pass to Nyame's destiny.

express their belief in their God and his works through proverbs that remind them constantly of his power.

AFRICAN RELIGIONS AND THE ORAL TRADITION

The African oral tradition, with its myths, legends, stories, and proverbs, instills the important elements of religion and culture in the minds and hearts of the African people all the way across the continent. The stories, myths, and tales that they hear and repeat from early childhood teach them about the ethics, beliefs, and traditions of their community. From their oral literature they learn why things are as they are and how life is to be lived on this Earth. Perhaps most importantly they learn of the power and majesty of a God, the Supreme Being, and of their special relationship to him, their Creator and the giver of all life.

CHAPTER 3

THE SUPREME BEING

I n the Adinkira patterns of Akan art, there is a pattern that is called Gye Nyame, meaning "Except God." When it appeared on a Ghana postage stamp, it was called "The Omniscience of God," referring to God's quality of omniscience, or knowing all things. A stamp collector remarked: "How apt that an African country should be the first to remind the world of God's power [on a stamp]." "Except God" is an end of a proverb that goes, "No one saw the beginning, none shall see the end, *except* God." That is to say that no one saw the beginning of creation, and no one will see its end, except God. (In Noel Q. King, *Religions of Africa*.)

Most African oral traditions have pointed to the existence of a power above which there is no other power, a Supreme Being, Creator, and Originator of the World.

THE AFRICAN CONCEPT OF MONOTHEISM

In Western religion religious systems are usually classified as either monotheistic, that is, believing in one God, or polytheistic, believing in many gods. In African religion monotheism and polytheism exist side by side.

A spirit ceremony is held by the Fon people of Benin, Nigeria, to contact the spirit world. In African traditional religion the spirits are always present, and requests and offerings are made to them for health, prosperity, and protection.

Often the African concept of monotheism is one of a hierarchy with a Supreme Being at its head. In this system the Supreme Being rules over a vast number of divinities who are considered to be the associates of the God. African understanding of the structure of the heavenly kingdom might be compared to the Christian concept of God ruling over the saints and angels. The divine hierarchy in African religion makes it possible to classify them as both monotheistic and polytheistic at once (monotheism with polytheism).

THE NATURE OF THE SUPREME BEING

How the many different African peoples conceive of God usually follows the social structure of a particular locality or culture. African people whose cultures are organized as monarchies with a king at the head usually conceive of their God as the supreme king. As there can be only one supreme king in a community,

Kente cloth, made by the Ashanti people of Ghana, is woven exclusively by men in narrow strips with complex patterns. The warp and weft threads that run up and down the cloth are each given names that symbolize beliefs, historical events, and political or community organizations. There are names such as dependency on God, progress, harmony, warmth, and bravery.

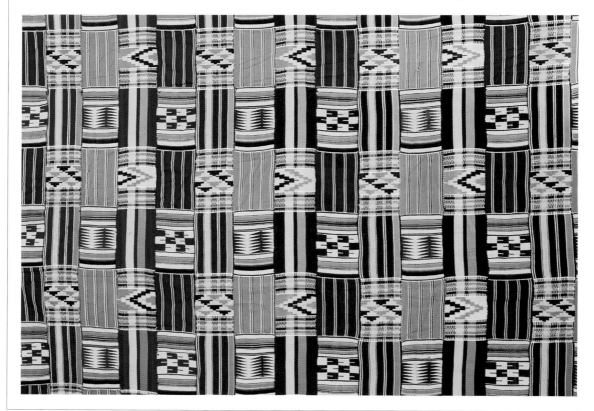

Africans have traditionally concluded that there can be only one Supreme Being for the entire human race.

The majority of African peoples conceive of God as one. However, among the Fon people of Benin in West Africa, Nana-Buluku, the name for God, expresses one God in duality, or two. In the Fon religion God is two beings, male and female.

The most complex concept of God is that of the Bambara people of West Africa. The Supreme God of the Bambara is called *Bemba* or *Ngala*. Bemba has, in a way, created himself as a quarternity (a union of a group of four). The four aspects of Bemba are Bemba, Nyale, Faro, and Ndomadyiri. The Bambara people understand these aspects of their God to be pure creative energy that is expressed as four "persons." Each plays a different role in the creation of the universe. This concept of a single God having a multiple nature is somewhat similar to the Christian doctrine of God as a trinity, or three in one—father, son, and holy spirit.

ATTRIBUTES OF GOD

People in African religious traditions frequently associate their Supreme Being with certain basic attributes. These are:

- God is the Creator of all things.
- God is the absolute controller and sustainer of the universe.
- God provides for what he created.
- God possesses all that he created.

The Aspects of Bemba

The Supreme Being of the Bambara, Bemba or Ngala, is one God in four. As the Supreme Being, he is master of all creation. Yet he has created himself in four aspects. They are:

- Bemba, master of air
- Nyale, also known as Mousso Koroni Koundye, master of fire
- Faro, master of water
- Ndomadyiri, master of Earth

Together as one, the four aspects of Bemba rule all of the elements on which life is based.

Nyame Symbol

Nyame, biribi wo soro, ma no meka me nsa ("O God, there is something above, let it reach me"). "This pattern was stamped on paper and hung above the lintel of a door in the palace. The King of Ashanti used to touch this lintel, then his forehead, then his breast, repeating these words three times." It is sometimes stamped on sheepskin or leather.

(In J. B. Danquah, *The Akan Doctrine of God: A Fragment of Gold Coast Ethics and Religion*.)

The Originator

The Banyarwanda of Rwanda in Central Africa speak simply of creation by saying, "There was nothing before God created the world." In the same region the Baila of Zambia call God "Creator." The Baila name is derived from the verb that means "to make, to originate, to be the first to do anything." So God is thought of as the Originator of all things. The Ngoni people of Southern Africa call God as Creator "the Original Source," and the Zulu of South Africa believe that God "made all things"; pointing to heaven they say, "the Creator of all things is in heaven." The Banyankore of Uganda in eastern Africa refer to God as "the Creator who sets things in order, creates everything and gives new life," while the Akan of Western Africa refer to God as "He who alone created the world."

THE CREATOR OF ALL THINGS

Both African oral traditions and later written sources indicate that all African peoples believe that power of creation is the foremost attribute of the Supreme Being. African myths of creation strongly support the idea that all Africans at all times from prehistory to the present-day have recognized a Supreme Being as the Creator of all things. In addition the names by which many different groups across Africa call the Supreme Being express the idea of God as the "Originator," Creator of everything.

CONTROLLER AND SUSTAINER OF THE UNIVERSE

In most African tradition and thought one's God has absolute control of the universe and all that it contains. This is because all other beings exist because of him. As Originator of the universe, God is the ultimate fountainhead of all power of all natural rules for orderly existence.

Peoples of the different regions of Africa express God's controlling and sustaining role of creation in various ways. The Ashanti of Ghana in West Africa regard God as the "Supreme Being, upon whom men lean and do not fall." The Nandi of Kenya in Eastern Africa believe that God "is the far-off driving force behind everything, the balance of nature." The Bambuti of Congo in Central Africa express the control and sustenance of God in the saying "If God should die, the world would also collapse," which expresses their belief in the controlling and sustaining power of God. From South Africa the Zulu say that God "made us, and is, as it were, in us his work. We exist because He existed."

THE PROVIDER

In names, in mythology, in legends, and particularly in proverbs, African people show that they are aware that their God provides for them. They acknowledge this in a variety of ways.

The name for God among the Ovimbundu of southwestern Africa means "He who supplies the needs of his creatures." In expressing the basis of God's providence, the Baganda of Uganda in eastern Africa have a proverb: "God gives his gifts to whosoever he favors." Africans have also observed that the providence of God functions entirely independently of human beings. The Ewe of Ghana in western Africa say that God "is good, for he has never withdrawn from us the good things which he gave us"; the name by which the Bakiga know God means "the One who gave everything on this Earth and can also take it away."

Snow-covered Mount Kilimanjaro is the highest mountain on the African continent. Such mountains, including Kenya, Elgon, Cameroon, and the Rwenzori Range, are regarded as seats of divinity.

THE POSSESSOR OF ALL HE CREATED

In many African traditions God is not only the giver of life, he is also the possessor of whatever has been created. The Barundi of Central Africa have two names that describe God as "the Owner of everything" and "the Owner of all powers." The Baganda of Uganda in Eastern Africa call God "the Master of all things." The Nuer of Sudan in North Africa neither grumble nor complain when a person or a cow dies, but simply say that God "has taken only what was his own."

A totem in a street in the town of Possotome in Benin. A totem represents a spirit that offers protection to an individual, family, or community. Totems can represent animals, plants, or natural phenomena such as lightning or flowing water, and their strength and power flows into those protected by it.

THE NAMES OF GOD

The following names of God express African ideas of the One God the Creator. These African names demonstrate the unity of thinking about a God while at the same time expressing the African diversity of expression about the same and one God. The names listed are all taken from Africa south of the Sahara Desert, where living African religion is found. They represent different regions, countries, and ethnicities.

Central African Regions

Country	Ethnicity	Name	Meaning
Burundi	Barundi	Imana	The Creator of everything
Cameroon	Bamum	Njinyi	He who is everywhere; He who sees and hears everything
	Bulu	Mabee	The One who bears the world
	Duala	Ebasi	Omnipotent Father
Central African Republic	Baya	Zambi	Creator
Congo (Brazzaville)	Vili	Nzambi	Creator and ultimate source of power
Congo (Kinshasa)	Baluba	Vidye	Great Creator Spirit
Gabon	Fang	Nyame	Creator
Rwanda	Banyarwanda	Imana	The Creator of everything
Zambia	Ambo	Leza	Creator
	Barotse	Nyambi	Creator
	Baila	Leza	Creator

(continues)

Eastern African Regions

Country	Ethnicity	Name	Meaning
Kenya	Akamba	Mumbi	Creator, Maker, Fashioner
Sudan	Nuer Dinka Shilluk	Kwoth Jok Juok	Creator Spirit Creator Spirit Creator Spirit
Tanzania	Chagga Gogo Nyakyusa Bazinza	Ruwa Mulungu Kyala Kazooba	Sun Creator Owner of all things Power of the Sun
Uganda	Baganda Alur Banyankore	Katonda Jok Ruhanga	Creator, Originator Creator Spirit Creator and Fixer of everything

Western African Regions

Country	Ethnicity	Name	Meaning
Benin	Fon	Nana-Buluku Mawu-Lisa	Original Creator Continuer of Creation
Burkina Faso	Tallensi	Wene	Sky God
Gambia	Serer	Rog	Creator
Ghana	Ashanti	Nyame	The Shining One
Ivory Coast	Akan	Onyankopon	Alone, the Great One

Country	Ethnicity	Name	Meaning
Nigeria	Igbo Yoruba	Chwuku Olodumare	Great Spirit The Most Supreme Being
Senegal	Serer	Rog	Creator
Sierra Leone	Mende Kono	Leve Yataa	The High-Up One The One you meet everywhere

Southern African Regions

Country	Ethnicity	Name	Meaning
Angola	Bacongo Ovimbundu	Nzambi Suku	Creator He who supplies the needs of His creatures
Botswana	Tswana	Modimo	The Greatest Spirit
Lesotho	Basuto	Molimo	The Greatest Spirit
Malawi	Chewa Ngoni	Mulungu Uluhlanga	The Creator The Original Source
South Africa	Zulu	Unkulunkulu	The Great Oldest One
Swaziland	Swazi	Mvelamqandi	"Who-appeared-first," the power above, unapproachable, unpredictable, of no specific sex
Zimbabwe	Shona Ndebele	Mwari Unkulunkulu	He who is in, or owns the sky, the Great One of the Sky The Great Oldest One

CHAPTER 4

THE SPIRIT WORLD

In African religion the Supreme Being reigns as the chief god in heaven. However, in most traditions he is not involved in the day-to-day affairs of human beings. This function he delegates to the less important gods of African belief who occupy the spirit world. The spirit world is made up of superhuman beings, beings that occupy the spiritual universe between gods and humanity, the space between heaven and Earth. They invisibly tread the Earth so that they are continually present. It is to these lesser gods that people turn in times of joy and sorrow. It is to them that they make requests concerning their needs and desires, and to them that they make offerings and sacrifices for health and happiness, successful crops, the birth of healthy children, and protection from evil.

Superhuman beings exist in a hierarchy—that is, they are ranked according to their nearness and importance to the Supreme Being. The most important superhuman beings may be called associates of God. These are lesser gods who rank below

A Dogon hunter next to the bones of the animals he has killed. The Dogon have a close relationship with the spirits of the animal kingdom, and Dogon hunters were traditionally the members of the tribe who left the protected world of the village to learn what lay beyond. This original role of the hunter is still celebrated in the music and dance of the Dogon.

the Supreme Being but who often work jointly with him. Other influential spirits of the community are intermediaries, guardians, and ancestors. Intermediaries are spirit agents that act as go-betweens between divinities and humans. Spiritual guardians and ancestors are protectors and advocates for humans, spiritually positioned between superhuman beings and human beings.

SPIRITS OF THE SPIRIT WORLD

African tradition and thought consider spirits to be elements of power, force, authority, and vital energy underlying all existence. Invisible though this power may be, Africans perceive it directly. People know and believe that spirits are there. In their daily lives they point to a variety of actions that verify the existence of spirits. They also know that spirits are to be handled with care. Hence the variety of rituals and taboos that acknowledge the existence of spirits.

Spirits are found everywhere. And where they are considered to be, people feel their presence. There is no object or creature, there is no corner of the Earth, that is not inhabited by spirits. The more something commands awe—by its size, beauty, or power—the more that thing becomes identified with spirits.

SPIRITUAL GUARDIANS

Spirits, no matter at which level they may be, inspire some sense of superhumanity. One example of this is those spirits designated as spiritual guardians. Spiritual guardians are a varied group. Among them are ancestors and the spirits of departed heroes. Another type of spirit resides in natural landmarks. A nearby mountain may be the abode of the spirit that is guardian to the community. The spirit of a river may be identified as guardian of that area. An extraordinarily huge tree in a village may be considered the abode of a local spiritual guardian.

Protection from Enemies

The Galla people of Ethiopia and Kenya in East Africa call on spiritual guardians of the community for protection against enemies with the following prayer:

If enemies would come,
let not your small worm die,
but stretch your hand over him.

AFRICAN TRADITIONAL RELIGION

Animal life, too, may house spirits. A leopard may be accepted in a community not as a mascot, but as a spiritual anchorage of the guardian spirit of a locality. Guardian spirits of a community are

A guardian figure of the Kota people of Gabon in Central Africa dating from the early 20th century. It consists of a copper and brass plate attached to wood. It serves to protect the local community and is a focus for prayers and sacrifices.

Crossing to the Spirit World

Among the Edo people of Nigeria, when someone dies senior family members speak prayers at the burial. One such prayer is the following:

Your children whom you have left here, you should order money for them. You should send them children. You should send them everything That is used in the world . . . As they have lived to do this for you. Let their children live to do it for them . . . As you looked after your children. When you were in the world, So you should look after them Unceasingly.

SPIRITS OF THE DEPARTED

The spirits of the dead are part of the spirit world. Some are ancestors and others are the spirits of the ordinary dead—that is, the dead of the community who are neither ancestors nor identified as outstanding members of the community. Africans do not worship their dead ancestors, but they do venerate and respect them. The ordinary dead are respected as well, with due ritual observations by all the members of the community. In African religious belief, when a person dies his or her soul separates from the body and changes from being a soul to being a spirit. Becoming a spirit is a social elevation. What was human becomes superhuman. At this point the spirit enters the state of immortality. The living are expected to take note of this development and render due respect to the departed through ritual.

People expect ancestors to be unceasing guardians of the living. The Edo people of Nigeria bury their dead with their feet pointing west, toward the Ughoton, the old port of Benin on the West African coast. From Ughoton the dead are believed to embark in canoes and cross the sea to the spirit world that lies in the dome of the sky.

African Polytheism

The term *polytheism* is derived from two Greek words: polus, meaning "many," and theos, "god." With regard to African religion, it means a system of belief that recognizes and venerates many gods. These are the gods with a lowercase g, who are also described as associates of a Supreme Being, a God with a capital G.

THE SPIRITUAL HIERARCHY

Imagine the universe as being like a government. At the head is the Creator, the Supreme Being. He is ever present but does not manage the daily affairs of human beings. This responsibility he delegates to

A traditional healer in South Africa uses a snake skin as a magic charm to bring health and success. Traditional healers have extensive knowledge of medicinal herbs that they combine with a knowledge of spiritual and mystical forces.

A *sangoma*, or traditional diviner, using charms to interpret or forecast events in KwaZulu–Natal, South Africa.

his associates—also divine, but of a lesser order. The associates of God are spiritually made to head departments. These gods have been brought into being as functionaries in the God-centered government of the universe. They are the divinities who do the spiritual work of managing the human world, and they are the ones people call on in times of trouble. They are local gods, intimately connected with local situations. Each of them is the god of a particular people with a specific function in ordering the total life of the community. Under their various names and functions the divinities form the pantheon of gods in each particular locality. Pantheon is the term for all the gods of a particular people taken together. The pantheons of the different African religions differ somewhat according to the needs and character of the people.

THE YORUBA PANTHEON: ORISA

The Yoruba are a Nigerian ethnic group of 12 million people with a rich religious tradition. At the top of their religious ranking is Olodumare, the Supreme Being. Next are the associates of God known as divinities, gods, or deities. These are ranked according to the importance of the function they oversee. Next are the spirits of ancestors and those of the ordinary dead. The pantheon of Yoruba gods is known as the Orisa. It has a membership of as many as 1,700 divinities. Examples of a few of the most important follow.

ORISANLA

Orisanla or, as he is sometimes called, Obatala, is the second in command in the Yoruba pantheon. Yoruba tradition refers to Orisanla as the offspring of Olodumare. He has many of Olodumare's attributes,

Iwa

Among the Yoruba, morality is summed up in the word *iwa*, which can be translated as "character." *Iwa*, according to the Yoruba, is the very stuff that makes life a joy, because it is pleasing to God. Orunmilla once sought the means of success in life and was told that the only way was for him to marry Iwa. He accordingly married Iwa and became very successful.
The Yoruba people say:

Character is all that is requisite.
Character is all that is requisite.
There is no destiny to be called unhappy in Ife city.
Character is all that is requisite.

(In E. Bolaji Idowu, *Olodumare: God in Yoruba Belief.*)

and Olodumare has delegated creative powers to him. As Olodumare's deputy, he created the Earth and its arrangement as well as the physical part of human beings. For that reason he is called the "Maker."

ORUNMILLA

Orunmilla is the Yoruba god of divination, the practice of seeking to discover future events or hidden knowledge in one's life by consulting the superhuman world. The Yoruba believe that Olodumare has endowed Orunmilla with special wisdom and foreknowledge, so anyone wishing to know the future may consult Orunmilla through his priest, known as a *babalawo*. Yoruba tradition provides divination in a form known as Ifa, which Yoruba religious devotees consult before undertaking anything important.

ESU

Esu is the most complex of the Orisa. He contains both good and evil properties. Esu's function is primarily that of a "special relations officer" between heaven and Earth. He is the "inspector general" who reports to Olodumare on the actions of other divinities and those of human beings. Esu investigates, checks, and reports on the correctness of worship and sacrifices. Because of his assignment as inspector,

Music usually accompanies African religious ritual and is used in prayer to request favors or help from the spirit world. The drum unlocks communication with the spirit world.

Esu may be found everywhere, checking on the spiritual orderliness of the community.

Esu's dual nature of good and evil, together with the role of corresponding as mediator between heaven and Earth, makes

him a "trickster" figure, a kind of mischievous superhuman being. He is believed to hold the power of life and death, depending on the kind of reports he makes to Olodumare. Consequently Yoruba people seek to be on good terms with him. They venerate him whenever they venerate any other Orisa. Because of this Esu has a place in every shrine.

People strive to be on good terms with Esu by being constantly vigilant. They try to avoid anything that may annoy him. For example, should some mishap occur, they are quick to make good what may have gone wrong. They also make sure that Esu's portions of sacrifices are duly offered to him.

OGUN

Ogun is another associate of God who ranks high in the Yoruba pantheon. He is the divinity of war and of iron. Ogun exists on the edge of society. He is as hard and tough as steel, and all iron and steel are his spiritual possessions. He rules over oaths, covenant making, and the cementing of pacts. In local courts, instead of swearing "to speak the truth and nothing but the truth" by holding the Bible or the Quran, Yoruba people take oaths by kissing a piece of iron, usually a machete, in recognition of Ogun's spiritual authority.

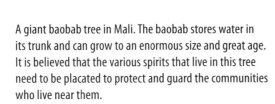

A giant baobab tree in Mali. The baobab stores water in its trunk and can grow to an enormous size and great age. It is believed that the various spirits that live in this tree need to be placated to protect and guard the communities who live near them.

Ogun is recognized as the patron of warriors, hunters, artisans, blacksmiths, goldsmiths, engineers, mechanics, barbers, butchers, truck and taxi drivers, and ironworkers of all kinds. Such people often visit Ogun's shrine in search of spiritual assurances for their work.

JAKUTA AND SANGO

The expression *the wrath of God* is represented by the gods Jakuta and Sango. Jakuta is one of the lesser divinities of heaven, whereas Sango is believed to have once been a human being who was raised to the status of a divinity. Jakuta literally means "the one who fights with stones" or "the one who hurls stones," and originally the commandments against stealing, falsehood, and poisoning were his.

Jakuta and Sango are regarded as coworkers in creating lightning and thunder. The Yoruba have such a sense of their God's wrath that during a thunderstorm people who have reason to fear God begin to tremble. It is in this sense that Yoruba tradition regards Jakuta and Sango as being functionaries of God's ministry of justice.

THE BAGANDA PANTHEON: LUBAALE

The Baganda are an ethnic group of Uganda. Their pantheon is called Lubaale, or beings from Olubaale, the dome of the sky. It contains about 70 divinities. They know the Supreme Being as Katonda, which means "Creator." The Baganda speak of Katonda as the father of the gods, because he created all things. While some Baganda divinities are connected to nature, the majority are hero or ancestor gods who have been raised to the status of divinity.

GGULU

Literally, *Ggulu* means "sky," "heaven." It is the name both of heaven and of the sky god. Ggulu is thus the divinity next to Katonda, the Supreme Being. In Buganda lore the wife of the founder of the Buganda kingdom was the daughter of Ggulu, who came to Earth from heaven with her brother Walumbe. The Buganda people originate with her, and therefore from heaven.

KIWANUKA

Kiwanuka means "something that descends at a great speed." Kiwanuka is god of thunder and lightning. He is also a god of fertility whom couples consult when they wish to have a child. When their prayers are successful parents often name their child for the god: Kiwanuka for a son, or Nakiwanuka for a daughter.

KITAKA

Kitaka is believed to be Mother Earth. The king consulted this divinity in cases of capital punishment so that the spirits of the dead would not return to harm him. People also consult Kitaka about cultivating the land, in order to have abundant crops.

WALUMBE

The literal translation of this god's name is "Mr. Death." Walumbe is the son of Ggulu, the sky god, and the brother-in-law of Kintu, the first king of Buganda. When Walumbe's sister, the king's wife, made the mistake of forgetting to bring some provisions to Earth and went back to the sky to fetch them, Walumbe, her brother, returned to Earth with her. Since then Mr. Death has lived in the underworld as the divinity of death. A temple to him, built and cared for at Tanda in Uganda, reminds the population of the existence of death.

WANGA

Wanga is one of the oldest of the population of the deified heroes of the Baganda. These "terrestrial gods," lower ranking than the "sky gods" who rule in heaven, are the ones to whom the Baganda turn on a daily basis with their prayers and concerns. In the traditions of the Baganda people, the Sun once fell from the sky. The king called upon Wanga. He rose to the challenge and restored the Sun in its place in the heavens. As a reward the king allotted an estate to Wanga and built a temple there. People consult Wanga about sickness and disease. He also foretells how people may turn aside calamities and troubles that befall communities.

MUSISI

Musisi is the son of Wanga. His name means "earthquake." The Baganda people turn to him during natural calamities such as earthquakes.

MUKASA

Mukasa is a deified hero of the Baganda. Of all the superhuman beings within the Lubaale who invisibly populate the Earth and are in daily contact with humans, he ranks highest. People turn to Mukasa with concerns for health and fertility.

KIBUUKA

Kibuuka, the brother of Mukasa, is the war god of the Baganda. Consultation regarding warfare and national defense is directed to him, together with his nephew Nende, also a divinity of war.

THE FON PANTHEON: VODUN

The Fon pantheon is known as the Vodun. *Vodun* may mean "god" in the sense of a divinity, and it may also mean a pantheon. Vodun worship is the religion of the Dahomey, or Fon, people in West Africa. All of the Fon gods are members of the Vodun, including the dead, who are elevated to the level of gods. The Vodun includes both the great gods and also lesser gods who stem from the greater pantheon.

The great gods are included in three pantheons. These are the Sky Pantheon, the Earth Pantheon, and the Thunder Pantheon. The Supreme Being of the Fon, Nana-Buluku, rules over all as the Originator, Creator of the beginnings of the universe. Priests of the Fon religion teach that Nana-Buluku was at once both male and female. This Creator is also believed to be the parent of Mawu-Lisa.

THE SKY PANTHEON: MAWU-LISA

Mawu-Lisa is a complex god whose most striking feature is a dual nature. This twin god was born to Nana-Buluku, the Creator, who also represents the duality of female and male. Mawu is female, associated with aspects of the world that relate to the Earth, the west, the Moon, the night, and the rising Sun. Lisa is male, representing the sky, the east, the Sun, the day, and the setting Sun.

In addition to representing the dualities of the physical world, Mawu-Lisa symbolizes opposing aspects of human life. Mawu, the female principle, reflects fertility, motherhood, gentleness, and forgiveness. Lisa, the male principle, reflects strength and toughness. Mawu-Lisa together expresses the unity and duality of the physical world.

THE EARTH PANTHEON: SAGBATA

The deity Sagbata is known as the "king of the Earth." Sometimes he is referred to as the "owner of the soil." According to tradition veneration of Sagbata arose after an epidemic of smallpox. Thus Sagbata came to be the divinity who protects against smallpox.

THE THUNDER AND THE SEA PANTHEON: SOGBO

To the people of Benin the sea, thunder, and lightning represent mysterious forces that are seen in terms of superhuman powers. Therefore anything to do with thunder and the sea is addressed through the pantheon whose head is Sogbo.

THE FON PANTHEON OF LESSER GODS

Among the Fon pantheon of lesser gods, the most notable include Legba, the divine trickster; Se, the souls of man; Fa, fate and divination; and Da, the cult of the serpent. Legba was the youngest of the 12 children of Mawu-Lisa. When they divided the universe among their offspring there was no domain left for Legba. Instead

A traditional mask from Benin in West Africa worn during the Gelede ceremony. The masks are worn by men during a ritual performance that takes place between March and May at the beginning of the new agricultural season. The ritual pays tribute to the special power of women elders and ancestors. The lower mask depicts a woman's face and the upper part of the mask often depicts humans or animals such as birds or snakes. In African religion each ethnic group has its own deities, spirits, and ancestors; in addition there are local spirits or guardians that may be linked to a village or a family.

they gave Legba the role of messenger between his siblings and parents. Legba's domain is therefore communication. Nothing happens without his awareness. Importantly, Legba conveys the wishes and desires of human beings to the Vodun.

People sacrifice to Legba, fearing that if he does not receive the sacrifices he demands he can prevent the Vodun from hearing their supplications. However they also mistrust him, and they may hold him responsible for the misfortunes of life. They also characterize him as a trickster. However, Legba is an important figure in determining the fortunes of human beings, who can normally approach Mawu-Lisa only through him.

AFRICAN PEOPLES AND THE SPIRIT WORLD

Associates of one's God, natural spirits, the spirits of departed heroes, ancestors, and other members of the community all join together to create a sense of living in a spiritually charged universe. For African believers the spirit world is never very far away. It is present in sky and sea, Earth and all creation, and in the memory of those who have gone before. People feel communion with the spirits all around them and communicate with them regularly through sacrifice, offering, worship, and simple conversation. The gods of African religion are as near to them as their family, friends, and neighbors.

CHAPTER 5

RITES AND RITUAL IN AFRICAN RELIGION

To Africans belief without ritual action would take away much of religion's natural power. Rites and ritual punctuate all aspects of African religious life. Religion is so deeply ingrained in the daily life of traditional Africa that it is all but impossible to separate it from other aspects of the culture. In an African community religion is the strongest influence on people's thoughts, acts, and lives. Rites of passage and other communal rites are the clearest examples of how religion permeates all aspects of African life.

RITES OF PASSAGE

Rites of passage are rites that have to do with the human life cycle. They are practices, customs, and ceremonies that people perform to move people smoothly through the stages of life from beginning to end. These stages include birth and childhood, puberty and initiation, marriage, aging, and death.

In Eastern Cape Province, South Africa, a young Xhosa boy, his body smeared with gray clay, sits in the bush as part of a manhood initiation rite. Every year, thousands of Xhosa boys go to the bush for about four weeks to become men. They are usually circumcized the first day and are not allowed to eat for the first seven days.

"GOD'S WATER"

A tradition of the Banyarwanda and Barundi of Central Africa illustrates the idea of God's participation in conception. They have a custom and rite known in their language as Amazi y'Imana, which means "God's Water." They keep a little water in the house at night. Every woman who hopes to bear a child will always make sure that the water is there before she goes to bed. Starting from the moment of conception, Imana, or God, is supposed to use the water in his work of creation.

The religious reliance on God and other superhuman powers only becomes more important when a couple fails to conceive. Then they turn to the designated divinities in charge of fertility. The couple and their supporters approach the divinities with prayers and sacrifices as a means of requesting the favor of pregnancy. When the favor is granted and the woman announces that she is pregnant, there is rejoicing. Both spiritual and medical precautions are taken to ensure normal pregnancy and delivery. Those involved offer a sacrifice to the Supreme Being, the national gods, or the ancestors and guardian spirits, who have an interest in seeing that the community continues through the birth of new members.

BIRTH AND CHILDHOOD

The early stages of the life cycle include conception, the period of pregnancy, the actual birth of the child, its naming, and its childhood. The rites of birth begin with the mother's pregnancy. Some African traditions regard conception as a cooperative venture between the parents-to-be, their God, and the associate gods.

PREGNANCY

When the time for the birth comes, experienced elderly women act as midwives to help the mother deliver the child. The role of midwife is considered the sacred calling of a medicine woman. In African religion healing is a religious activity. The birth may take place in the house or nearby in a secure area of the garden.

Along with the newborn baby, the placenta and umbilical cord receive special consideration. These two items, so closely related to the newly born, require religious care. The ritual disposal of the placenta and the umbilical cord indicates that the child has died to the state of pregnancy and is now alive in another state of existence. The child is born into the new life as part of human society.

BIRTH SPIRIT

The Baganda of Uganda believe that a child is born with a double, or twin, called a *mulongo*. This twin consists of the placenta and umbilical cord. After the birth the mother wraps the placenta in banana leaves and buries it at the foot of a banana tree in such a way as to protect it from wild animals. The tree then assumes

A mother and child of the Himba people living in northern Namibia. In African traditional society a child is delivered by a midwife, who is usually a medicine woman considered to have healing powers.

TABOOS

African people consider a pregnant woman to be chosen for a duty—motherhood—that is a sacred calling. She is therefore subject to a variety of taboos. A taboo is the custom of putting someone or something under prohibition. The pregnant woman is encouraged and sometimes instructed to refrain from various activities. Some taboos have to do with her diet. During pregnancy women are forbidden salt, because it may harm the child's skin. Eggs and pork are also taboo in order to protect the child's appearance and shape. Other taboos regulate the woman's personal habits on religious grounds or to check her sexual behavior. All are aimed at bringing about the safe birth of the child, though there are also in some cultures underlying and increasingly contentious issues of the role of women and their autonomy.

Igbo Names Honoring God

Chukwudi, "God lives"
Ifeanyichukwu, "nothing impossible with God"
Chukwunwke, "God creates"
Kenechukwu, "thank God"
Chukwuemeka, "God has been very kind"
Chukwuka, "God is great"

sacred significance until the fruit matures. When the bananas ripen the child's paternal grandmother uses them to prepare a sacred feast marking the occasion.

In addition the mother preserves the part of the umbilical cord that remains attached to the child after birth. It is believed to contain a protective spirit. When it drops off she wraps it in bark cloth and preserves it. At the time of the child's naming it is dropped in a container of banana wine, milk, and water. If it floats the child is considered legitimate, and the naming proceeds. If the cord sinks the child is considered illegitimate, and the mother is punished.

NAMING THE CHILD

The name a child receives is expected to express the very essence of the person who bears it. Names individualize children, give them a standing, and incorporate them into the community. Parents take much care, therefore, in name giving.

Naming ceremonies in Africa differ from people to people, but the names themselves have a number of things in common. All African names have specific meanings. Most African personal names at least indirectly reflect religious belief, and some have strongly religious themes. Countless personal names in African religious traditions express religious ideas. Some are connected with divinities, and many are related to spiritual and human circumstance. Others relate to attributes of the Supreme Being. For instance the Luo-speaking people of Kenya, Sudan, Tanzania, and Uganda frequently name children Ojok, related to Jok, or God. The Igbo parents of Nigeria honor Chukwu—that is, God—by naming their children in praise of his power.

FROM PUBERTY INTO ADULTHOOD

Puberty rites are ceremonies performed to mark the time during which young people move from childhood to adolescence. They initiate young people into the adult world, marking the physical changes that signal the transition from the asexual world of childhood to the sexual world of adulthood.

INITIATION

The approach, timing, and places for the rites of initiation vary from people to people. Young people may be initiated through either physical initiation or instructional retreats. Physical initiation usually means circumcision, or the removal of the foreskin of the penis for boys, and an operation to remove the clitoris for girls. This so-called female circumcision is now an issue of deep controversy. Its antifemale emphasis and the not-infrequent deaths caused by this painful operation on young girls have led to international agencies and many traditional elders demanding that the practice cease. Yet it has also now become an issue by which hard-line traditionalists express their opposition to modern trends such as the rights of women.

Apart from their drama and impact, initiation rites convey many religious meanings. Elders take young people to retreats away from home where they learn the arts of communal living. They

Ashanti Prayer for a Girl's Puberty

At the time of a girl's first menstruation her mother pours a little wine on the ground and speaks this prayer:

Nyankopon Tweaduapon Nyame
(Supreme Sky God, who alone is Great)
upon whom men lean and do not fall,
receive this wine and drink
Earth Goddess, whose day of worship is
a Thursday, receive this wine and drink.
Spirit of our ancestors, receive this wine
and drink.
This girl child whom God has given
to me, today the Bara (first menstrual
period) state has come upon her.
O mother who dwells in the land of
ghosts, do not come and take her away.
And do not have permitted her to
menstruate only to die.

(In Robert S. Rattray, *Religion and Art in Ashanti*.)

are introduced to the basic facts of adult life. They are taught the sharing of privileges, rights, duties, and responsibilities of the community. The initiation rites give them instruction in matters of sexual life, marriage, procreation, and family responsibilities. Through this initiation they are prepared as adults to shed blood for their people. They are also encouraged to accept the responsibility of planting their biological seed as a way of contributing toward a new generation of the community through marriage.

MARRIAGE

Marriage is a starting point for a new generation, as it is a starting point for personal immortality through offspring. In African thought marriage is a religious obligation. Without marriage there is no assurance of having descendants. The departed count on being taken care of by, and are assured of being reincarnated or reborn through, their descendants. A person who has no descendants in effect disrupts the chain of reincarnation, to the great annoyance of the superhuman beings. Marriage therefore is a sacred undertaking that must not be neglected.

The families gather in a wide circle. The men, wearing Zulu costume, dance. Then there is an exchange of presents from the

In Bedik village, Senegal, Bassari boys encircle a hut where an initiation ceremony is taking place to mark a young man's transition into adult life.

A ZULU WEDDING

Before a couple marry, their families negotiate the traditional bride payment, or *lobola*. People believe that the groom respects the bride more if he must pay for her. Traditionally the *lobola* was paid in cows, but now it is usually paid in cash. After the groom pays the *lobola*, there are other ceremonies in which gifts are exchanged. At the end the groom receives a sheep or a goat. This gift shows that the bride's family has accepted him.

Early on the wedding morning the groom's family slaughters a cow, which is cooked and eaten for the wedding feast. The bride's family watches, making sure that the meat is divided equally between the two families. They sing and exchange gifts. In the afternoon the bride arrives. She wears the traditional Zulu costume with a leopard-skin neckpiece and a beaded hat and skirt. With her family carrying her hope chest, she tours the groom's property. This symbolically introduces her to the groom's family.

bride to members of the groom's family. These are usually blankets and mats. The recipients dance or sing their thanks. The groom's gift, a blanket, comes last. It is presented to him in a skit, where it is thrown over his head. The bride's friends beat him playfully, indicating what they will do if he does not treat the bride well, until he escapes. With the exchange of gifts over, the feast begins. The feast seals the marriage. When the two families have eaten together the couple is joined as one.

AGING

As they advance in age people are deemed to grow in experience and wisdom. Parents are expected to bear the torch that helps enlighten the young. They take part in the expectations as observed in the African proverb "It takes a village to raise a child." In time they come to old age and qualify to be addressed as elders, among whom are found the sages and seers of the community. However, in recent decades there has been a decline in traditional respect for the elders due to such factors as the move from rural to urban areas and the resulting weakening of family structures. In addition many families have been broken up by deaths caused by the AIDS virus, civil strife, or natural disasters. There is also the influence of a growing global youth culture accessed through improved communications such as the Internet, with an emphasis on consumerism rather than traditional values.

DEATH

Death is the time when the soul leaves the body to become a spirit. African mythology allots a great deal of space to the subject of

death. Usually the same myths of creation that trace the origin of human beings include the origin of death. In these myths death often comes to the world because of human misdeeds. Although African people accept death as a natural part of the life cycle they generally feel that each individual death always has a cause associated with supernatural powers. These include mystical powers like magic, witchcraft, and sorcery. The understanding of death brings with it the realization that a person's body and soul are no longer one. In dying, the individual has joined the world of the departed. This fact usually evokes sorrow for those left behind. A spiritual period of mourning sets in, with funeral rites that vary by ethnic group.

Members of the Karamojong of northeastern Uganda carry a portable granary along the road near Kotido town. The granary is given by the bride's family as part of her dowry when she marries.

Death calls for a ritual disposal of the body of the deceased. Burial rites are performed by the community. Those attending the burial bid farewell to the deceased by throwing a bit of soil or flower petals into the grave before the burial is completed. People are very attentive to giving the departed a proper funeral. It is important that the spirit of the departed be content in the world beyond and not come back as a dissatisfied ghost to plague those left behind.

In many African traditions there are final funeral rites. These mark the end of the time of mourning. At this time the designated heir of the deceased is officially declared, installed, and invested with the ritual instruments that entitle him or her to the inheritance. Connected to the final funeral rites is the idea that the deceased may be reincarnated, or reborn, into a new life through naming. During this time the deceased becomes increasingly identified with the world of the spirits among whom he or she now dwells.

RITUAL

Rituals are religiously meaningful acts that people perform in appropriate circumstances, usually following strictly prescribed patterns. Rituals are the concrete expression of belief. African believers, and indeed believers of all religions, feel that they have to show their belief in some way. They do this by worshipping the Supreme Being, by doing reverence to superhuman beings, and by paying due respect to their fellow humans.

Prayer, music, and dancing enhance the effectiveness of ritual acts. Sacrifices and offerings help to confirm the relationship between the Supreme Being, superhumanity, and humanity. Rituals take place during community celebrations and festivals for the purpose of thanksgiving, purification, and communion. Their performance helps to link humanity with superhumanity.

PRAYER

In African religion there are countless prayers. Like other African religious literature they are handed down orally from generation to generation. Many prayers are traditional and centuries old. Most are recited by people in official capacities. These include priests and priestesses, diviners, rainmakers, medicine men and women, kings, chiefs, ritual and family elders, and heads of organized groups such as hunters. Prayers are usually addressed to God, superhuman beings, and ancestors.

People in search of spiritual assistance for a variety of human needs address their prayers to the powers above. People pray for life, health, healing, wealth, and prosperity. They pray for success at work. They pray to be delivered from difficulties. They address prayers either directly or indirectly through intermediaries for all spiritual assistance possible. They pray in praise, they pray in joy, and they pray in thanksgiving.

MUSIC

Music is an audible expression of African prayer. There are many religious songs in praise of one's God and superhuman beings. There are many songs intended to express joy for spiritual blessings. There are songs asking favors from above. And there are songs exuberantly sung in thanksgiving. Songs are usually accompanied by the beating of drums and the playing of other instruments.

DANCE

Whereas song is religious expression in voice, dancing concentrates on expressing religious emotions, elegance, and dynamism through bodily movement. African

---

Let Us Lift Our Voices in Prayer

Let us lift our voices in prayer,
Offering up an ox to the Creator.
May this ox be permitted to grow old,
That we may gain good health.
Let us lift our voices in prayer,
Offering up an ox to the Creator.
The Creator of the sky gives us peace.
Gives us food.

(In Alfonso M. Di Nola and Patrick O'Connor, *The Prayers of Man.*)

"Let a Fruitful Year Come upon Me"

In preparing the field a farmer in Ghana brings offerings of a fowl and cooked yam for the spirit of the Earth and for his ancestors. As the blood of the fowl drips on the Earth and the yam he says, "Grandfather (mentions the name), you once came and hoed here and then you left it to me. You also, Earth, Ya, on whose soil I am going to hoe, the yearly cycle has come around and I am going to cultivate; when I work, let a fruitful year come upon me, do not let a knife cut me, do not let a tree break and fall upon me, do not let a snake bite me."

religious ritual would be lifeless without the accompaniment of music and dancing. These are powerful means of African religious expression.

SACRIFICE

Sacrifice is giving up something valuable in order to render homage to some superior being. A sacrifice is thus a gift offered to God or to a superhuman being in recognition of their superiority over humanity. Of all acts of worship to the Supreme Being, sacrifices and offerings are emphasized most in African religion. The Abaluyia of Kenya refer to God as "the One to whom sacred rites and sacrifices are made." Animal sacrifice is the usual way of offering praise. Bulls, goats, or chickens are the most common objects of sacrifice, offered at every stage of the rites of passage.

COMMUNAL RITUAL

Prayer, music, songs, drums, other musical instruments, dancing, and sacrifice come together in vividly orchestrated communal ritual. These rituals celebrate such things as purification rites, communion rites, and agricultural rites.

BRINGING RAIN

Agricultural rites have to do with the way people use land for the production of food. Farming is one of the greatest preoccupations of the people. Its importance requires the blessings of God and those of the superhuman guardians of the people. For that reason each stage of agricultural development calls for spiritual assistance. Most important is the need for rain. Rain is so vital that there are certain rites, and ritual specialists, whose main function is to bring about rain at crucial times.

PLANTING AND HARVEST RITES

There are also rites concerned with the preparation of new fields, planting rites, and harvest rites. At the time of sowing and harvesting, African religious traditions have important communal ceremonies that link the people's agricultural activities with the

Dogon masked dancers from Mali performing
the Dana dance. The Dogon believe that this
dance creates a bridge into the world of the
spirits. Their masks are believed to have
magical powers.

A cow slaughtered at the marriage of Princess Nyawo to Nkose Tembe, king of Tsonga, in KwaZulu–Natal, South Africa. During the ceremony, which took place on April 3, 2004, the princess ceremonially assisted in skinning the cow to mark her entrance into the royal family.

spirits of the community. When the land is tilled and planted people of all African cultures ask blessings from the superhuman beings. At the time of ripening and harvest they hold "first fruits" ceremonies.

According to tradition, superhuman powers must eat of the first fruits of harvest before human beings partake of them. They must receive their share in offering before anything is given to anyone else. To deprive them of their important place in the hierarchy would induce them to take revenge by threatening the future harvest. The first fruits ceremonies are festival times for offering thanksgiving to the superhuman powers for the new harvest.

RITUAL LEADERS

Ritual leaders are those members of the community who preside over and conduct particular religious rituals. They come to their leadership roles in different ways. Some positions are hereditary. Others are the result of a special spiritual calling along with special training. This category of African ritual leaders includes rulers, priests, mediums, diviners, healers, rainmakers, elders, and sages.

RULERS AND LEADERS

African kings, queens, and chiefs have both privileges and duties. Their position carries with it outstanding power, authority, and influence. However although rulers are endowed with power and prerogative, they are also bound by obligations and kept in check by taboos. The ruler is the father/mother of the people and the symbol of their ethnic unity. He or she must therefore solve human problems and give an ear to all subjects, as well as representing the people in contact with other powers.

In many countries where African traditional religion is strong, the king is the high priest of the people. As high priest he is not only in charge of matters of government, but also of religious matters. For example, in Buganda, part of Uganda in East Africa, the veneration of the national gods is under the immediate control of the *kabaka,* or king. By his authority temples are built to the different gods. He has the ultimate power to confirm or reject the choice of priests made by the clans according to the traditions surrounding the different gods.

Besides being the primary religious leader of the people, the ruler is closely connected with ritual traditions. Ritual occasions connected with kingship or chiefdom, such as coronation, enthronement, and funeral rites, connect strongly to the sacred-

A Himba chief with members of his family in the Kunene region of northern Namibia. African people consider the authority of their leaders to come from their God. Their rulers are political leaders, but they are also true religious leaders. In African traditions there is no such thing as separation of church and state. Religion and human affairs, such as politics, by African religious standards go hand in hand.

ness of the ruler. Rulers are regarded as a God's earthly representatives. They are the reflection of the God's rule in the universe. To many African peoples rulers are not ordinary men or women. They are living symbols of the connection between the Supreme Being, the superhuman beings, and the human beings.

PRIESTS

In African religious tradition a priest is a ritual leader who oversees, administers, and coordinates religious matters for the com-

Father of Mysteries

In some African traditions the work of diviners is so revered that they are elevated to the position of divinities. For instance in the Yoruba religion the diviner is known as the Father of Mysteries, with no less a spiritual patron than Orinmilla, the Yoruba deity of divination.

People usually become diviners either by training or by inheritance. Diviners-to-be are privately trained by experienced diviners. In many cases the training period may last from three to seven years. They must master the oral tradition, which involves memorizing names and signs of divination as well as figures, proverbs, and stories connected with them. They learn to use the instruments of divination, including pebbles, seeds, gourds, numbers, and cowrie shells. They also learn how to read animal entrails, to read palms, to form images or use images in pots of water, and to interpret sounds.

munity. Priests may be men or women. Priests are key figures in maintaining the religious affairs of an African ethnic group.

Priests are usually attached to a temple of a god and are charged with its care. People become priests by both vocation and training. However, there are a few African societies like the Baamba, the Banyankore, and the Basoga of Uganda, the Bavenda of South Africa, the Binawa and the Srubu of Nigeria, and the Sonjo of Tanzania, in which priesthood is hereditary. People believe that priests and priestesses are called by the gods. Some are said to

Sangomas, or traditional diviners, gathered to perform a ritual at Saltpeter Cave, near Clarence, eastern Free State, South Africa. These diviners are believed to have the skills to read hidden signs about the past, present, and future.

MEDIUMS

Mediums are people who can contact the spirit world, usually by being possessed by spirits. As a rule they become mediums through being possessed by superhuman beings, after which they undergo training. Mediums are usually women. They are attached either to a priest at a temple or to a diviner. They sink into a trance, usually induced by music, drumming, and singing, and become possessed. The spirit speaks through the medium, transmitting messages from the spirit world to human beings. Sometimes the message may be in a strange language, and the priest or an assistant may be called to interpret.

have been set aside from birth. Others are said to have been called by a god through being possessed by his or her spirit. At other times parents send a child to be trained as a priest because the child was born in answer to prayer, and so is dedicated to the service of the gods. Trainees are submitted to the guidance of an older priest. Training is usually arduous. It may last some years, during which the child learns the secrets of serving a god.

DIVINERS

Diviners are ritual leaders whose special position is to unveil the mysteries of the past and future. In so doing they pronounce what may be causing problems in the community. Diviners not only read the signs of the present but also have techniques by which they discover hidden knowledge about the past, the present, and the future of those who consult them. To find out the unknown for a client diviners may use shells, pebbles, water, animal entrails, and many other objects regarded as "mirrors." From these they read why something has gone wrong.

HEALERS

In some parts of Africa a healer is called *musawo,* "a person with a bag." Healers are easily distinguished by the bag they carry and by their attire. Healers customarily wear amulets, shells, and other decorative accessories that ordinary people do not wear. The bag that they carry is their trademark. In it are all types of medicines. In a broad sense healers are ritual leaders whose service relies on supernatural powers. They come to the aid of the community in matters of health and well-being. Healers work in conjunction with other ritual leaders to keep the members of the community physically and spiritually healthy.

In African thought illness is always caused by superhuman agencies or by extrahuman forces such as magic, witchcraft, and sorcery. Therefore someone who is sick must determine the spiritual cause of an illness in order to cure it. Answers to the question of why an illness has occurred may come from the spirit world in oracles or divine pronouncements through the cooperation of a priest and a medium. Or they may come from the superhuman and extrahuman world through the cooperation of a diviner. Oracles and divination are the means of identifying the cause of illness and the illness itself. When the illness is identified the healer can devise the cure. Healers then turn to the spirit world for help in getting and administering the right medicine.

Healers are often specialists. Some focus on performing healing rituals in combination with other ritual leaders. Others may concentrate on one aspect of healing such as bonesetting, herbal remedies, or dietary prescriptions. Their specialties depend on how the healer received his or her calling. Some healers are healers by inheritance. Their craft is handed down from parents or relatives. Others learn the trade from experienced healers with whom they study and work for a substantial length of time before they are allowed to practice on their own.

These powers can also be used to bring suffering, by cursing someone who is thought to be behaving in an inappropriate way. Fear of such curses and belief in their efficacy is widespread throughout Africa and can cause real distress, mental breakdown, or even death. Its role is intended to be one that places the safety of the community above the safety of the individual.

RAINMAKERS

Rain, so essential to agriculture and therefore to survival, is closely connected to African religion. Rain is viewed as divine

MEDICINE MEN AND WOMEN

Healers are variously referred to as medicine men or women, herbalists, and sometimes as witch doctors. They are some of the most influential people in an African community. Their influence comes from their important work of curing members of the community of illness and disease. Their gifts are both material and spiritual. Materially they have wide knowledge of healing herbs and medications. Spiritually they heal the underlying spiritual causes of illness.

influence that descends to Earth. The continued fertility of the land requires rain. When it fails to fall people begin to wonder what they may have done wrong. They feel a need to put right whatever has caused a problem between them and the Supreme Being or the spirit world. They call for the ritual leadership that comes from those known as rainmakers.

Rainmakers are specialists in religious matters pertaining to rain. They determine the reasons why rain fails to fall or why there is too much rain. Rainmakers perform rites of prayer or sacrifices offered to ensure that enough rain will fall at the proper times. They also preside over prayers and sacrifices offered to check excessive rainfall. They are thus both rainmakers and rain stoppers.

A person may become a rainmaker either by training or by inheritance. Through messages from the spirit world and through dreams a person may find a call to become a rainmaker. Then that person may train under an experienced rainmaker. A fairly

African women herding livestock in a canyon in Debre Libanos, Ethiopia. Rural life and the survival of livestock and crops is dependent on the rains, which is why the role of rainmaker is highly regarded.

"GOD'S BLESSINGS ARE FALLING"

The Dinka of Sudan know their chief deity as Deng or Dengdit, which literally means "rain." The Kikuyu of Kenya know their key god as Ngai. Ngai has three capacities. By the first he sends rain and riches, by the second he sends good wives and healthy children, by the third sickness and loss. It is in the first capacity that Ngai is considered to be the Supreme Being and is credited with divine powers. The Churi and Masai of eastern Africa and the Ewe of western Africa say of rain, "God is falling" or "God is weeping." Other African people say "God's blessings are falling."

long period of training is required before the person can enter a serious practice.

There are also rainmakers who achieve this religious and ritual position by inheritance. Most renowned of these is the queen of the Balovedu of southern Africa, who is called a "rain queen." She is not primarily a ruler, but a rainmaker. People rely on her for their security not in regard to regimentation, armies, and organization, but on her power to make rain for them and to withhold rain from their enemies.

CHAPTER 6

SACRED SPACES AND PLACES

The places where the rites and rituals of African religion are carried out are African sacred space. Some of these places are constructed specifically for religious purposes, but others are natural places in the environment where people come together for ritual purposes. There are also places that would normally be regarded as nonsacred but that may on occasion serve as ritual spaces. These are often homes in which senior family members may officiate as ritual elders.

SACRED SPACE

Some places are made sacred through the relics of divine beings. For example, the Uganda Museum in Uganda is only a museum to the general visitor. However since British colonial times relics of the local gods have been confined there. For local people this building is therefore a sacred space. When they visit the

The Kasubi Mausoleum is a huge thatched burial place of four kings of Buganda in Uganda. Religious functions are held there around the time of the new Moon throughout the year. Built on the outskirts of Kampala, the capital of Uganda, it attracts many local and international visitors.

AFRICAN TRADITIONAL RELIGION

museum they do so with care and with a sense of awe and mystery. So a museum visit becomes a casual sort of ritual. The gods may also signal the special sanctity of a place in some way. Animals, by their symbolic relationships to the gods as well as by their ritual guardianship of a locality, often are signs of communication from the spirit world. Their appearance in a certain locality may mark that place as sacred.

In a larger sense people understand the whole land of their particular culture and ethnic group to be sacred. The narratives of the sacred origins of the land and its people communicate this sacredness. For this reason present-day political leaders who ignore the sacredness of a people's lands often become the cause of unrest.

SPIRITUAL GEOGRAPHY

Africans have long associated the wonders of nature with religion. In African tradition anything that seems to be shrouded in mystery has tended to evoke a sense of the religious, and the natural world is filled with beauty and mystery.

For African people the whole universe is filled with religious spirit. In African religion all elements of the universe are regarded as symbols of the divine. The sacred space of the universe has three parts. Above the Earth is the sky, or heaven, the home of the supreme being. Below the Earth is the realm of the spirits, which keeps humanity connected to the land.

In the middle is the Earth, the world of humanity and the here and now.

THE SKY

The African sky inspires much religious feeling. High in the heavens the blazing Sun and glowing Moon inspire humanity with awe. The night sky is embellished with thousands upon thousands of twinkling stars that, on a clear night, can leave observers in a state of wonder.

Sun, Moon, and Earth carry aspects of divinity. Among African peoples in all corners of the African continent, the Sun is a symbol of the Supreme Being. In general the Moon is recognized as a natural phenomenon that carries sacredness, serenity, and tenderness. For that reason Africans mark the appearance of the new Moon with rituals that express the sacredness of the Moon.

THE NATURAL WORLD

The Earth, too, is a source of wonder. Africa's geography is extremely varied. Natural landmarks include mountains, oceans, lakes, rivers, waterfalls, forests, rocks, caves, and trees, any or all of which may inspire religious feelings. The forest and plains are alive with a great variety of animals: chattering birds, creeping reptiles, spiders, and insects, all of which, by inhabiting the world with humans, beg the question of their place in the universe.

RITUAL PLACES AND OBJECTS

For Africans ritual places are human-made structures or marked areas at which religious rites may be observed. These include shrines, tombs, temples, and sacred localities. Since the beginning of time Africans have sensed a great invisible power, a vital force that surrounds and is

SACRED MOUNTAINS AND HILLS

Although almost any geographical feature in Africa may become the focus of worship, mountains and hills are the features usually identified as being sacred. The people who live near the great African mountains such as Mount Kilimanjaro, Mount Kenya, the Rwenzori Mountains or the Mountains of the Moon, Mount Elgon, and Mount Cameroon, make sacrifices and offerings, perform rituals, and offer prayers to the Supreme Being and other spiritual powers on or beside such places. Other natural sites such as trees, islands, lakes, rivers, and waterfalls may also be designated as sacred spaces.

THE MAGIC OF GREAT ZIMBABWE

The name "Great Zimbabwe" is given to ancient stone ruins in the country of Zimbabwe. These ruins, which include massive walls, a stone tower, an acropolis, or cluster of buildings on a hilltop, go back many hundreds of years and testify to Africa's ancient culture.

I think the place is well over a thousand years old. Somewhere some day we may argue the case. Here is where we redeem the half promise. Any book about the magic of Africa that did not include a word about the Great Zimbabwe, as it is called, would be unthinkable.

The first thing which strikes one is the large expanse of ruined stone dwellings, huddled together at a respectful distance from the great buildings of the temple and fort, reminding one irresistibly of the silent City of the Dead sprawling in its solitary decrepitude under the serene gaze of the Sphinx.

(In Frederick Kaigh, *Witchcraft and Magic of Africa*.)

A section of the Great Zimbabwe, massive stone ruins dating back a thousand or more years. Traditions of the Shona people of Zimbabwe, who worship Mwari as the Supreme Being, connect religious practices to the Great Zimbabwe.

part of all nature. To help themselves come to terms with this power Africans have devised ways of containing it by inviting it to reside in human-made places and objects, so that they may perceive it in smaller doses.

Places built for religious purposes may be temples and other constructed shrines. Temples are architectural structures that vary in size and shape. Other constructed shrines may vary from a pillar or monument to a small stone or an iron or wooden marker. Examples of such shrines include the Staff of Oranyan and the Central Shrine of the powerful Ogun in Ile Ife.

TEMPLES

A temple is a place or a building where people congregate to worship, to pray, and to ask for favors from spiritual powers. There are numerous types of temples in Africa constructed according to the various traditions of different peoples. There are large temples, small ones, and even miniature ones. Many have been overwhelmed by the appearance in Africa of religions like Christianity and Islam, but others have persisted and have been adapted to contemporary colonial types of architecture.

Temples in other parts of Africa, built by the people and attended by priests and priestesses, often follow the pattern of local construction. In the kingdom of Buganda in Uganda these may be conical and thatched. Some Nigerian temples, like the Obatala and the Ifa temples of Ife, represent African religious temples built on the basis of Western architectural influence. One of the most conspicuous temple buildings in Africa south of the Sahara is connected with Great Zimbabwe. This is a stone building of complex construction possibly devoted to the worship of Mwari, the Shona name of their Supreme Being, and cults of the *mhondoro,* the spirits associated with the ruling dynasties in this southern African area.

Shrines

In African religion a shrine is any container, box, or receptacle that may receive and contain superhuman power. A shrine is therefore an anchorage, or place of rest, for spiritual powers. As a constructed structure, in addition to natural landmarks, a shrine marks the sacred geography of a religious tradition.

An *akuaba* figure is a symbol of fertility for the Ashanti people of Ghana. They are carved as wood statuettes and worn by girls and women to assure childbearing.

TOMBS

The tradition of tomb building in Africa goes back millennia, including tombs such as the pyramids of ancient Egypt and Nubia. Helping us to trace back some vital religious ideas, the Great Pyramids at Giza express belief in divinity of the king as representative of the Sun god Re and the place where he ascended to join the Sun god in the afterlife. There are many other representative types of religiously expressive tombs, among which are the Kasubi Tombs of the Kabakas of Buganda in Uganda. These tombs are tended by young priestesses, who keep the fires within them and perform rites that worshippers may attend. The tombs thus serve as places where ordinary people may be in touch with the higher powers.

MARKED LOCALITIES OF RELIGIOUS SIGNIFICANCE

In many African religious traditions there are localities that are identified as shrines without the construction of elaborate buildings or structures. For example, the shrine of Ogun, a Yoruba divinity considered to be one of the most powerful as the chief blacksmith in heaven and a bloodthirsty hunter on Earth, is a locality in Ife marked by stumps of wood and by stones. It is at such a shrine that his followers, who include hunters, blacksmiths, engineers, mechanics, drivers, artisans, and all people who deal in iron, steel, or other metals, go to seek spiritual help.

RITUAL OBJECTS

Ritual objects such as talismans or statues are used in observing African religious rites. The use of ritual places and objects goes far back in African tradition. Ritual objects are comparatively small human-made items. One such item is a shrine object, a small amulet or charm that is believed to carry spiritual power. These objects may be produced in a multitude of forms. They may be owned communally or personally. Other religious objects are usually works of art with religious themes, such as masks or statues of gods. They may also be items intended for utilitarian purposes, like pitchers or pots, which because of religious decoration or form may spontaneously be considered religious objects.

Sculptures as Ritual Objects

Lacking writing, Africans carried their mythology—their literature—in their heads, transmitting the legends orally from generation to generation. Sculpture was an additional language through which they expressed their inner life and communicated with the invisible world, a language of emotional communication, used from birth to death. Virtually every act in the life of the African had its ritual, and every rite had its appropriate image.

(In Ladislas Segy, *African Sculpture Speaks*.)

SACRED SPACE IN AFRICAN LIFE

At home, in temples and shrines, and in the countryside, African people are aware of the sacredness around them. Although they may congregate in a particular place or turn toward a particular geographical feature during prayer, they have a continuing sense that superhuman beings walk beside them in their daily lives. Their presence makes all places potentially sacred. Sacredness may be more concentrated in a place built or designated as such, but in fact it is everywhere. The objects that African people create and place on shrines and in their homes are continuing reminders of this sacredness.

CHAPTER 7

MYSTICAL FORCES

African people feel the power and energy of the spirit world that is all around them. They experience the actions of gods and ancestors in everything they do. African people are deeply aware of the powerful force of creation that put them on the Earth and guides their footsteps. They are closely attuned to the mystical and mysterious superhuman powers in their lives. In addition to their sense of the vital force of the universe, Africans recognize other types of forces that are neither superhuman nor simply human but lie somewhere between. These mystical forces include magic, witchcraft, and sorcery. Like spiritual forces, they affect people's lives and the lives of their community.

MAGIC, WITCHCRAFT, AND SORCERY

Magic is the practice of manipulating mysterious forces for practical purposes. People who are able to bring about magic are known as magicians. In African belief magic is a far cry from the smoke and mirrors of the Western theater stage. African magic does not have to do with illusion or trickery. It is a true religious

A traditional healer selling medicines and herbs in Durban, KwaZulu–Natal, South Africa. The healer's practice of medicine combines knowledge of medicinal herbs with spiritual and mystical forces.

element. Africans believe that magic is neutral. It may be used for either good or evil purposes. African religion is mainly concerned with asking the cooperation of one's Supreme Being and superhuman beings for the well-being of humanity. In the sense that ritual leaders are able to call upon the higher powers effectively, there is always something of a magician in the personality of a ritual leader.

Magic in African religion, as in many other religions, makes the unknown less threatening and provides psychological reassurances for potentially difficult or even dangerous situations. Although Westerners do not call it magic, there are many things people do, often without knowing they are doing them, that an African would consider to be magic at work. They believe it is magic when a baseball player crosses himself before stepping up to the plate in order to get a hit. It is for magical protection that a truck driver places a rosary on the dashboard. Ritual acts and talismans provide magical protection from unknown dangers around the world.

RECEIVING THE GIFT OF MAGIC

To the peoples of Africa magic and religion are so closely related as almost to be one. The Ewe of Ghana believe that God sent magic power into the world after he had created the first person. The Langi of Uganda add that the art of magic originated partly in God and partly in the spirits. However, they are not certain as to when this took place. The Azande of Sudan note that the art of magic, together with the knowledge of making medicines and the ability to avenge crimes, were given to humanity by God. The Bemba of Central Africa simply say that magic is a gift from their God. Behind these beliefs about magic is the general belief that God is the Creator of everything, including this puzzling force of magic.

WITCHCRAFT

Traditionally African people believe that witchcraft is one of the causes of misfortunes in a community. Witchcraft is a dreaded element in African society. People define witchcraft as the state of being possessed by extrahuman forces that can do evil or harm. A sizable population of Africans at all levels of society believe in witchcraft. They hold witchcraft responsible for such misfortunes as failure to bear children, diseases, failure in life, illness, and death.

People have a variety of views about how someone becomes a witch. The most commonly belief is that the trait is inherited from a parent. In that sense some people

A *sangoma,* or traditional diviner, throwing animal bones to read hidden signs revealing events affecting an individual or community. *Sangomas* are often called upon to interpret community problems or disturbances.

Magic

In magic certain gestures, words, or acts, separately or together, are believed to invoke the direct assistance of supernatural powers in human affairs or to give people control over the secret powers of Nature. In another sense magic may be defined as the art of living in intimate union with Nature and sharing and using its secrets through ritual or "doing."

The profession of magician is held in esteem. It is passed on from father to son. As priest the magician promoted the welfare of the community; as medicine man he healed the ailing.

(In Ladislas Segy,
African Sculpture Speaks.)

The Magician and the Sorcerer

Although in the broadest sense the field of magic might be said to include sorcery . . . for the sake of simplicity we shall call magic that which is intended to have beneficial effects, and sorcery that which is intended to do harm. The magician mainly serves the community; he or she performs rites to promote fertility and avert misfortune. The sorcerer on the other hand is employed privately, serving one person in order to harm the enemy.

(In Ladislas Segy,
African Sculpture Speaks.)

are born witches. In the case of hereditary witchcraft it is possible for someone to be a witch and not know it, although eventually the witch notices his or her powers. These powers can be used to cast a spell and do harm to someone. Not all witchcraft is hereditary, however. People also feel that witchcraft can be "caught" like an infection, or that someone who wants to be a witch can buy the power from another witch.

Witchcraft causes evil and unrest in a community. The community fights its influence by calling on healers who specialize in curing the effects of witchcraft. These healers have come to be known as "witch doctors," a term that is often misunderstood both in Africa and in the wider world. Witch doctors are not witches themselves. That is, they are not evil people who want to harm their neighbors. They are respected members of society whose function is not to harm but to heal. A witch doctor helps those who believe they have been bewitched. The possibility of witchcraft is everywhere. People seek protection against it in a variety of ways. On the personal level they may use amulets, charms, or talismans to help ward off the presence of evil. A hunter, for example, may wear a piece of a tooth of a lion as protection against witchcraft during a hunting expedition. A pregnant woman may wear a talisman around her waist to protect her unborn child against witchcraft. The head of a household may hang an amulet on the doorpost of his house for protection of those within.

SORCERY

The *Oxford English Dictionary* traces the word sorcery to 1330 B.C.E. It means "the use of magic or enchantment; the practice of magic arts; witchcraft." To Africans, however, the "magic arts" are nothing artistic or enchanting. The African understanding of sorcery is as something darker and more dangerous. It is the use of magic to do harm. Sorcery shares this quality with witchcraft. The difference is in degree. Witchcraft may be defined as a mystical and innate power, which can be used by its possessor to harm other people, whereas sorcery is evil magic against others.

Sorcerers set out to do harm. Unlike witches, who may cast spells or call on mystical forces to do their mischief, sorcerers resort to artificial mean, such as poison to ply their craft. For example, they grow long fingernails in which to hide the harmful potions that they may drop in someone's food or drink. In African understanding sorcerers are evil. They cause much trouble in a community in the form of discontent, illness, and even death.

Some African societies specifically refer to sorcerers or sorceresses as "poisoners." Theirs is evil magic, deliberately aimed at harming people and communities. As in the case of witchcraft, people turn to healers for defenses against sorcery.

To African believers there is nothing imaginary about extrahuman forces. People believe deeply in the influence of these forces on their lives. Extrahuman forces are not to be ignored or taken

GOD'S CREATION AND PROTECTION

African people understand witchcraft to be part of the religious forces that surround them. The Nupe of Nigeria say that in the context of creation, "God also put the power of witchcraft in the world." The Barundi of Burundi add, "God gives power to the magicians and witches." But although witchcraft may be a creation of God, he also protects against it. The Igbo of Nigeria assert that "God punishes those who do evil and protects people against witchcraft." The Nyakyusa of Tanzania note that "God has the power to drive away witches." Witches are men or women who have within themselves the power to practice witchcraft.

Witchcraft and magic are related, but they are distinct from each other. The Azande people, for example, make a firm distinction between magic (*ngwa*) and witchcraft (*mangu*). *Mangu* is hereditary. It can be traced to a substance that can be found by autopsy in the stomach of a witch. It exerts a sinister influence over the lives of others in the community when it is roused by bad intentions. *Ngwa* is not identified with any special substance. It is divided into good magic and bad magic.

A Masai woman wearing jewelry, including protective amulets or charms on her ears, to help ward off danger or evil spirits. Women make elaborate colored beadwork traditionally worn as bangles and necklaces, while both men and women wear earrings that stretch the earlobes.

lightly. The following event, reported as fact, illustrates just how powerful these forces and the belief in them can be.

During the early 1960s an incident occurred through a combination of influences of superhuman and extrahuman powers. A husband and wife were quarreling. The situation deteriorated to the point that the husband consulted a medicine man. This medicine man, whose name was Kigangali, lived in a village called Mushanga, in the district of Ankore in Uganda. No ordinary medicine man, Kigangali was known for his remarkable command of mystical forces. Kigangali told the husband of Nzeera, the quarrelsome wife, that he would take care of the situation. Exactly what Kigangali did is unknown, but the effect of his magical manipulations was that Nzeera was turned into a lion.

Perhaps in the hope that she could be turned back into a woman through exorcism, people captured the lion and dragged it to the Christian parish center in Mushanga. Observers came from all over the area to witness what had happened. Before anything could be done, however, the lion died, and the woman's soul with it. The lion was buried with the rites due a human being; the woman was never seen again.

Almost 40 years later this extraordinary event is still discussed because of the sense of awe and wonder it created. To call down such powerful mystical forces is both terrible and wonderful, repellent and attractive. Yet those who believe in them have no doubt that such powers are real, and the changing of a woman into a lion is clear proof.

PROTECTION THROUGH PRAYER

People may seek protection from witchcraft for their community through prayer. The following is a prayer against witchcraft.

Be Good to Us

I offer thee this dege, this d'lo (nut), and this chicken in the sacrifice that I carry out in my name and in the name of my children.

Keep us safe from the suba (witches) o, from all evil and ugly spirits.

Be good to us, keep us from sickness, give us women, healthy children,

and take care to send us rain; give us physical vigor and in all ways preserve us that we may gather a bountiful crop.

(In Alfonso M. Di Nola and Patrick O'Connor, *The Prayers of Man.*)

CHAPTER 8

AFRICAN RELIGION IN TODAY'S WORLD

Throughout history people from outside the African continent have tended to misunderstand and to dismiss African religion, often because of stereotyping and prejudice. One clear indication of this is that until quite recently African religions were not considered "true" religions, not included on the list of world religions. Only lately has African religion received serious recognition as a world religion. The followers of Islam who established their influence on Africa's east coast in the 10th century called Africans *kaffirs,* or unbelievers. In the 15th century, when the Christians arrived, they accepted the term, and even went so far as to call the entire region Kaffraria. The idea that Africans were a people with no religion was widely accepted. African religious practices became known as fetishism—superstition and magic.

Celebrations at a gathering of the Nazareth Baptist Church in Gingindlovu, KwaZulu–Natal, South Africa. This indigenous Christian church has more than 700,000 members in South Africa. The church was founded in 1910 by a Zulu healer, Isaiah Shembe, who sought to infuse traditional African religion into Christianity. African traditional dance and music continue to be widely used in worship.

RECOGNITION AS A TRUE RELIGION

It took some 300 years for scholars to recognize African religion as a true religion. At first they called African beliefs and practices "primitive religion." This term recognized African beliefs as valid, yet "primitive" suggests something crude and unformed, whereas African religious practices were often highly refined. Eventually the religions of Africa came to be known simply as "African religion."

In 1957 Ghana in West Africa shook off the shackles of colonialism and became independent. This began a general movement toward independence in Africa. Political independence meant a return to African roots and a new appreciation of things African. It restored the "Africanness" of the African people. One outcome was that African religion experienced a comeback. By this time, too, the Western world had come to a greater appreciation and understanding of the value of African religion.

In the 1964 Vatican II Council, Roman Catholic bishops from all over the world met in Rome. They accepted African religion as a full partner among world religions. The influence of Vatican II spread well beyond the Catholic Church. Observers from almost all Christian denominations attended and carried its message back to their churches. They also quickly accepted African religion in its many manifestations as a full partner among world religions.

INFLUENCE ON RELIGION WORLDWIDE

African religion has great influence on African society and on African people throughout the world. All people of African heritage are tied to African religion by the bonds of culture. Their environment shapes their religious feelings and ideas. Although they may convert to other religions, people cannot give up their Africanness. It is too much a part of them. And a part of that Africanness is African religion. Even if they are Catholic, Protestant, or Orthodox Christians or Muslims, as many Africans are, they have formed their feelings about religion in general on the basis of their African roots.

African religion is deeply and fundamentally humanistic, centered on the human condition. This humanism colors all of life and its relationships. African humanism may be summarized in the principle of *Ubuntu*. *Ubuntu* is difficult to translate, but as South Africa's Archbishop Desmond Tutu, the Nobel Prize–winning churchman, has said, "You know when it is there, and it is obvious when it is absent. It has to do with what it means to be truly human, it refers to gentleness, to compassion, to hospitality, to openness to others, to vulnerability, to be available for others and to know that you are bound up with them in the bundle of life, for a person is only a person through other persons." This is the principle behind African religion. Ultimately this is the principle that empowers African religion to exert worldwide influence.

Archbishop Desmond Tutu, the Nobel Peace Prize winner, is recognized for his campaigning work on peace and justice issues not only within Christianity but among communities of many religious traditions and with secular governments.

KWANZAA

Kwanzaa is an African-American holiday. It was begun in 1966 by Maulana Karenga. This holiday pays tribute to the rich cultural roots of African Americans. *Kwanzaa* is an African word meaning "the first fruits of the harvest," and the holiday is based on African first-fruits celebrations. These are yearly celebrations with a fourfold purpose: To bring people together; to honor and pay reverence to the Creator and Creation; to commemorate the past; and to give the people the opportunity to recommit themselves to the highest ideals of the community. These ideals are summarized in the seven principles of unity, self-determination, collective work and responsibility, cooperative economics, purpose, creativity, and faith. Kwanzaa is celebrated annually from December 26 through January 1. Kwanzaa is usually presented as a unique holiday—not religious, political, or heroic, but cultural. However, as with all things African, it is impossible to separate religion from culture, and Kwanzaa carries religious associations along with cultural ones.

The ritual instruments of Kwanzaa festival include a straw place mat, a seven-branched candlestick, seven candles, a variety of fruits, a symbolic representation of the number of children in the home by ears of corn, a communal cup that represents unity, and a drink that is poured and shared together.

AFRICAN RELIGION IN THE AMERICAS

The influence of African religion goes beyond the African continent. In the Western Hemisphere, for example, elements of African religion appear in a number of local religious traditions. In Brazil Candomblé and Macumba are two religions whose backbone is African. In the Caribbean religions with strong African roots include Haitian Voodoo, which is based on the Fon Vodun worship; Cuban Santeria, a blend of African and Christian beliefs; Trinidadian Shango; and Jamaican Rastafarianism. Emigration has carried all of these to the United States. In addition traditions like the African Methodist Episcopal Church, which traces its beginnings to the time of slavery, incorporate elements of African religion.

INDIGENOUS AFRICAN CHURCHES

Within Africa people have adapted Christian beliefs and rituals to fit their own needs, establishing churches of their own. Many of these churches have strong elements of African religion. People felt that Christianity, with its emphasis on salvation in the next world, was not meeting their needs for the here and now. It did not, for example, offer protection against witches, ways of divining the future, and healing, which the new churches offer. The Aladura Church of Yoruba, with a membership of around 1.5 million, features leaders who act as healers and diviners. By some estimates more than 80 million Africans belong to the new churches; for example, the Church of Zion in South Africa has 5 million adherents and in Zaire, the Church of Jesus Christ on Earth through the Prophet Simon Kimbangu (Kimbanguists) has 7 million. Another factor in the development of the new churches has been people's need to shake off outside influences and take local control of their religion.

AFRICAN MUSIC

Music, either vocal or instrumental, usually accompanies African religious ritual. Music is used to praise the Supreme Being, the superhuman beings, and the ancestors. It is used as prayer in

supplication for favors from heaven. The drum is the primary instrument. It is a key that unlocks communication with the spirit world. People beat or play drums to induce oracles from high above, through mediums.

African Americans originated one of America's earliest original musical forms, the Negro spiritual. Negro spirituals, now familiar worldwide, were the creation of African Americans during the time of slavery. People sang them to express the grief and suffering to which they were often subject. The music soothed their own souls and those of their listeners. It presented religious, usually Christian, sentiments in a distinctly African style. From the United States to Europe and to the rest of the world, Negro spirituals have made a special mark on world music.

THE VISUAL ARTS

From their beginnings the people of Africa have expressed themselves through the visual arts. Rock paintings from ancient times have been discovered in many parts of Africa. Stone and wood carvings abound in African villages and homes. True works of art, they have found places in museums and in the homes of American and European collectors as well.

Singers at a community celebration in Nampula province, northeastern Mozambique. In traditional African religion instrumental or vocal music are used both in religious ritual and as an expression of community identity.

Originally all of these objects had a religious purpose. African religion is a religion without scripture and originally without written records. At one time people therefore concluded that it was a religion of illiteracy and without any kind of record. However in fact records of African religion are many. Some of the most important of these are its visual arts.

African visual arts have influenced some of the great Western artists of the 20th century. Among these were Pablo Picasso and Henri Matisse. Matisse recalled how an African statuette, with its strong character and purity of line, influenced Picasso's style and led to the birth of cubism, one of the most important movements of modern art.

AFRICAN RELIGION AND OTHER RELIGIONS

African religion is a vital part of the African heritage, and Africans who live on the African continent belong to that heritage. They are culturally connected to African religion. However, not all African people today claim to be adherents of African religion. Many of them are declared Christians, Muslims, or members of other religions.

Today leaders from other religions understand that they must first be able to talk meaningfully with others about the religion they have grown up in as well as the one they are adopting. Not long ago the missionary effort was aimed at erasing African religion from the African continent and the world. Today, however, the message is one of dialogue. That this is happening is a further assurance that African religion will continue to prosper. Far from being wiped out by the influx of other religions, African religion continues to thrive.

The Influence of African Religion on 20th-Century Visual Arts

It was the spirit . . . not merely African but universal, which was truly captured by modern Cubist artists. The fact that they collected African sculptures meant that these moderns lived with them sufficiently to absorb the sculptures' radiance, and not merely to "borrow" forms. They did not divide the form from the content, any more than the human body can be separated from the mind. It was an "influence," if one wishes to use this word; but an influence of the content which was first digested in its essence by the artists, and then recreated by them.

(In Ladislas Segy, *African Sculpture Speaks.*)

PICASSO AND SACRED ART

Pablo Picasso well understood the connection between African art and religion. He wrote, "My greatest artistic revelation came about when I was suddenly struck by the sublime beauty of the sculpture done by the anonymous artists of Africa. In their passionate and rigorous logic, these works of sacred art are the most powerful and beautiful products of the human imagination."
(In John Richardson, *A Life of Picasso*.)

A handmade wooden mask from Nubia, southern Egypt.

AFRICAN RELIGION AS A SUBJECT OF STUDY

Only recently has African religion become a serious subject for study. Early students of African culture tended to see only what they wanted to see—exotic ritual and mysterious rites that meant nothing to them. They reported on its color and strangeness, but without understanding. Since that time anthropologists, scientists who study humans and their societies and cultures, have conducted many studies of African religion that have promoted a better understanding. They have greatly contributed to assuring African religion a place among world religions.

During the late 1950s, along with African independence Africans developed a keen awareness of their religion. They began to study it as never before. Books and textbooks appeared on the subject. In the United States Harvard University inaugurated the teaching of African religion in 1977. Since that time African religion has become a popular subject of study at colleges and universities and at the high school level.

AFRICAN RELIGION AS AN ORGANIZATION

African religion is usually called a "traditional religion," one that is spontaneously passed down from generation to generation. It has not been considered an "organized religion" in the sense that it does not have an elected church leader, a church hierarchy, or elected officials to run the business of the church and rule on matters of doctrine. However, African religion does have an internal structure. It is first of all a dynamic and living religion. Its leaders regard their religion as a whole consisting of interdependently coordinated parts. In recent years leaders of African religion have begun to apply practices of organization and association to African religion. For that reason, today in Africa and in other countries where African religion exists, it is becoming increasingly organized.

Other aspects of African religion are becoming increasingly organized as well. One of these is healing. Practically all African countries have taken initiatives to establish organizations and associations through which members of the healing communities may work together, for example by exchanging notes for the material and spiritual well-being of the people. Organizations such as the Uganda Herbalists and Cultural Association in Uganda and the Traditional Doctors' Association in South Africa are two of these.

International drug companies are working to understand the healing knowledge that the medicine men and women possess, particularly with regard to healing herbs. In the invaluable knowledge of the African healers may lie the treasure that sets off the new "scramble for Africa."

Importantly for African religion, the knowledge and secrets of the healers cannot be cut away from their religious connections. There is the opportunity here for the knowledge and the secrets of the African healers to be preserved for the future but there is also a real risk. Outside organizations, especially multinational companies, are not interested in this vital link. How healing knowledge can maintain its religious ties in the face of this medical exploration poses a great challenge to contemporary African religion.

CHAPTER 9

AFRICAN RELIGION PAST, PRESENT, AND FUTURE

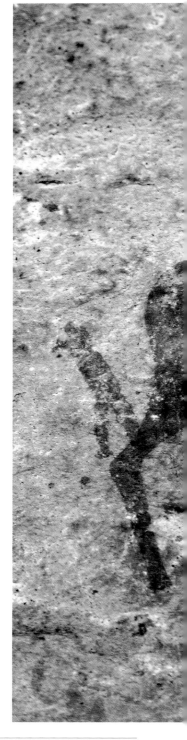

S tudy has shown that besides being rational, humans are also social and religious by nature. For ages inhabitants of Africa chose their elders to be their religious leaders and sages. These leaders and sages have been the custodians of and consultants to the religious needs of a community. And there is no reason to believe that such cornerstones of African religion will cease to exist in the near future. The influence of religion among Africans is powerful. Geoffrey Parrinder wrote that many colonialist administrators described Africans as an "incurably religious people." With this in mind the history of African religion can be organized in terms of precolonialist times, colonialist times, and postcolonialist times.

Prehistoric paintings of early San people (Bushmen) herding cattle, on the walls of a cave in the Cederberg region of South Africa. San rock paintings believed to date back 25,000 years have been discovered at more than 2,500 sites. The San were the first inhabitants of the Cape in South Africa.

In Latin *Africa* (i.e., *terra Africa*) means "the land of the Afri." This name designated only the area that contained the Roman province, while the rest of the landmass was simply considered unknown land. In Latin this unknown land was called *terra incognita*. The incorrect translation of that Latin phrase later became "the Dark Continent." Over time *Africa*—the name for the Roman province only—was extended to include the entire continent as we know it today.

The Antonius Pius arch of the second-century Roman city of Sufetula near present-day Sbeitla in Tunisia. The city was built on an area once inhabited by nomadic tribes, especially Berber people.

PRECOLONIALIST TIMES

African religion cannot be discussed without looking at the origins of the name *Africa*. From a geographic point of view *Africa* refers to the second largest of the seven continents. In early times, around 264–146 B.C.E., inhabitants of northern Africa lived within the borders of the political influences of the city-state of Carthage; they were known as Afri. In 146 B.C.E. the Romans conquered Carthage and coined a new name for the area: Africa.

The phrase *African traditional religion*, then, is meant to include the obsolete and the living religions of Africa. It includes the indigenous religions of Africans as experienced in all five regions of the continent of Africa, as well as the fundamentally basic units of the religious expressions of Africans. While the label *indigenous religions of Africa* refers to religions that originate in Africa, the five regions of the continent

In some areas of the African continent, especially in the north, indigenous religions became obsolete because they were no longer practiced. Egypt was home to a now-outdated ancient Egyptian religion; the Berber religion was found in the northern part of Africa, west of Egypt; the Cushite religion was practiced south of Egypt; the Aksumite religion in the southeast area of present-day Ethiopia. These religions have fallen into disuse for many centuries and are now obsolete.

represent the geographical bases of the diversity of African ethnicity. We speak of African religion both in the singular and in the plural. The singular represents the oneness of the religion of Africa as far as the spirit of the religion is concerned. However African religion can also be expressed in the plural with respect to the expressions of the religion of Africa by the many African ethnicities.

OLD AND NEW AFRICAN RELIGION

For a very long time before the colonialist occupation, people in sub-Saharan Africa practiced religion. The existence of those religions is evident in ancient African art—particularly in rock engravings and paintings, sculptures, and buildings—as well as in the traditions of African folklore. Both artistic objects and oral traditions were created to reflect the religious fabric of the people who created them. It is helpful to look at some examples in the different regions of sub-Saharan Africa.

ANCIENT EASTERN AFRICA

Eastern Africa is not known for ancient artworks such as rock engravings. It is, however, well known as the source of the Nile River. Peoples from Burundi to Egypt consider the Nile to be the personification of a river god. As such, they regard the river with religious admiration and respect. Also, contemporary eastern African paleoanthropologists such as Dr. Richard E. F. Leakey have publicized the region as the home of the "East African Man." Dr. Leakey's discovery of this important fossil has led many to regard eastern Africa as the place where humankind originated.

ANCIENT SOUTHERN AFRICA

African religion in southern Africa is expressed through oral tradition and art. Southern Africa has ages-old art records in the form of buildings and utensils. These are functionally related to the systems of beliefs and modes of thinking of the people of southern Africa. The San people of southern Africa have excelled in rock art in the form of engravings and paintings that reflect the life they lived long ago. Archaeologists, anthropologists, and art historians believe that the rock art of the San people was produced some 25,000 years ago.

ANCIENT WESTERN AFRICA

Several art forms—ancient sculptures in particular—give evidence to the rich religious expressions of the peoples of western Africa. A serious study of western African sculpture is likely to challenge the observer with a sense of religiosity revealed in the art. In 2002 the Metropolitan Museum of Art in New York City opened an exhibition of African sculpture titled "Genesis: Ideas of Origin in African Sculpture," and described the exhibit in this way: "The works relate to traditions that interweave elements of myth, history, religion, and contemporary experience to address universal questions: How did the world begin? What is our ancestry? What is the source of agriculture, kingship, and other societal institutions?"

In western Africa there are many traditions of sculpture that enshrine the spirituality and religiosity of the people. Perhaps the most visible of those traditions is that of the Yoruba people. Ile Ife, the capital of Yorubaland, is said to have been in existence since around 350 B.C.E. and is believed to be the center of the world.

One of the most impressive things in Ile Ife is the sculptured granite monolith known as Opa Oranyan, which means "the staff of Oranyan." As oral tradition has it Oranyan was the hero warrior and son of Oduduwa. Oduduwa was associat-

Ancestral Home and Holy City

The Yoruba people of western Africa believe that Ife is the center of the world. E. Bolaji Idowu, one of the most outstanding writers on Yoruba religion, summarizes the relationship between Ile Ife and Yoruba religion in the following way: "In order to reach the heart of the Yoruba in this way, the first place of importance for us to go is Ile Ife, their Ancestral Home, and their Holy City. After this, and only after it, should we look elsewhere. And so let us pay a visit to that Ancient City!"

(In E. Bolaji Idowu, Olodumare: God in Yoruba Belief.)

ed with Olodumare, the Supreme Being in matters that relate to creation. He is the progenitor of the Yoruba people and heritage that originate in Ile Ife.

Yoruba religious heritage has extended to many corners of the world. In particular it has made notable contributions to the cultures of Brazil, Cuba, and the United States. Many modern people recognize Ile Ife to be central to their roots.

ANCIENT CENTRAL AFRICA

Christianity, at its entry point in ancient Central Africa, testifies to the presence of African religion since ancient times. In 1491 King Nzinga of the kingdom of Kongo in Central Africa converted to Christianity through contacts with the Portuguese adventurers. He encouraged the Kongo nobility and peasants to follow his example. African Christianity lasted in Kongo for 200 years. The strength of African religion accounts for the swift embrace of Christianity by the people of the Kongo kingdom.

In African religion a king is not only a ruler; he is also a religious leader. When their king converted to Christianity it was obvious that his subjects would follow suit. The highly centralized and hierarchically structured society helped information flow throughout the kingdom. Christian doctrine was easily translated into Kikongo, the local language. Concepts like *god, spirit,* and *holiness* easily found equivalents with concepts in Kongo religion. Portuguese missionaries helped establish a spirit of cooperation.

COLONIALIST TIMES

The Portuguese exercised navigational prowess along the western and eastern coast of the African continent. What they saw of African religious practice in coastal areas led them to conclude that Africans worshipped fetishes. The interior of Africa, however, continued to remain a mystery to Europeans. Stories about the Mountains of the Moon, suppositions about raw materials in the interior of the continent, and pagans who remained unconverted attracted much speculation and attention in Europe. The situation encouraged Europeans to consider exploring the interior of Africa. Between 1768 and 1892, 10 European explorers went to Africa. Seven of these were British, one was French, one was German (working for the British government), and one was Anglo-American.

Europeans learned about Africa from the explorers and this knowledge led to European ideas about colonialism. (The term *colonization* refers to acts of settling on a given piece of land, while *colonialism* is the system in which a nation imposes its authority over other peoples' territory.) The European scramble for Africa that ended in the Berlin Conference of 1884–85 arbitrarily divided Africa among European colonialist powers. Colonialism left all parts of African native cultures, including religion, fractured and bleeding.

During colonialist times African religion was thought of as a "less-than" religion—on a par with paganism, fetishism, primitive religion, and animism. Before and during the times of colonialism African religion was dismissed as being unimportant to the development of modern society. And even to those with less critical views African religion was often tolerated rather than accepted.

POSTCOLONIALIST TIMES

By the time World War II began about 80 percent of the African continent was under European colonialist rule. During the war many African men were recruited into serving in the armies of the colonialist countries. African soldiers served in many different corners of the world for long periods of time. The length of their service and the experiences they gained made them think differently about the

DISMISSING BELIEFS

Under colonialism African belief systems and modes of thought became subjects of ridicule. Explorer Samuel Baker was among those who thought that African belief systems did not even exist. In an 1867 article ("Race of the Nile Basin") he said, "Without any exception [Africans] are without a belief in a Supreme Being, neither have they any form of worship or idolatry; nor is the darkness of their minds enlightened by even a ray of superstition. The mind is as stagnant as the morass which forms its puny world." Some colonialist administrators spoke with disgust about Africans, whom they called "these incurably religious" folk. Some missionaries wished to destroy what they thought of as devilish and superstitious beliefs and replace them with what they considered to be true religion.

A drawing of the Anglo-American explorer Henry Morton Stanley approaching Lake Tanganyika. In 1869 Stanley was commissioned by the *New York Herald* to search for the missing Scottish explorer and missionary David Livingstone, whom he finally found at Lake Tanganyika in 1871. In the years that followed Stanley continued to explore large areas of Central Africa.

future of their countries when they returned home. As war veterans Africans now had the knowledge and experience to work for the end of colonialism in Africa.

In 1945 the United Nations was formed to promote peace, security, and cooperation, and in 1948 it issued the Universal Declaration of Human Rights. Africans started demanding political independence from European colonialist administrators. In some cases Africans demanded the return of religious objects that had been sent to Europe. For example, the Baganda in Uganda demanded the return of the relics of Kibuuka, the Buganda god of war, from the United Kingdom. The relics were returned. In 1957 Ghana in western Africa was the first African country to gain political independence from the government of Her Majesty Queen Elizabeth II of the United Kingdom.

INDEPENDENT AFRICA

Colonialist administrators and missionaries had put many African religious practitioners under watch. As a result people practiced religion secretly and under the cover of the night. Many Africans practiced Christianity during the day while they attended African religious sessions at night. Political independence brought about change, however. It made people feel confident about themselves—not only politically, but also in terms of their relationship to African religion. Many postindependent African governments protected the practices of African religion and many African governments have declared African religions to be official religions.

EDUCATION AND RENEWED CONFIDENCE

Since independence many Africans have rediscovered the worth of their religion and have stopped feeling insecure about their religious heritage. Such insecurity was instilled in them by outside religious and colonialist rule that had viewed African religion as being inferior.

To deal with challenges and doubts about African religion, African leaders looked to education. Departments of religious studies were first introduced in the top universities in sub-Saharan Africa, including the University of Ibadan in Nigeria, the University of Ghana, the University of Sierra Leone, Makerere University in Uganda, and the University of Nairobi in Kenya. These institutions paved the way for the teaching of what came to be African Traditional Religion.

Catholic lay missionaries working on an educational training program with children in Nairobi whose parents have died from AIDS. Members of various religious traditions, including indigenous African religion, are increasingly working together in Africa on health and community programs.

ISLAM AND CHRISTIANITY IN INDEPENDENT AFRICA

The first outside religion to find its way into Africa south of the equator was Islam. Muslims first arrived in eastern Africa from southern Arabia in the eighth century. The newly arrived Muslims considered Africans to be unbelievers.

From the late 15th century onward Christianity began to arrive in sub-Saharan Africa. Long established in countries such as Egypt and Ethiopia, it was the European journeys of discovery starting with the Portuguese that brought Catholicism, and then from the 17th century Protestantism, to Africa. Many missionaries, both Catholic and Protestant, regarded as devilish anything that had elements of African belief. As John Baur states in his book 2000 *Years of Christianity in Africa*: "This was due to two misconceptions: on the one hand, there was the unfortunate but quite general European prejudice that Africans were a primitive people without religion; on the other hand it had become generally accepted in Europe that all magic and all spirits were devilish."

TOLERANCE, UNDERSTANDING, AND DIALOGUE

Both Christianity and Islam were essentially hostile to traditional African religion, destroying statues and shrines and overturning ancient customs as devil worship or as being of no significance any longer. In recent decades attitudes have changed, led in particular by the theological changes within the Catholic Church after Vatican II, which encouraged Catholics to see God within all religions; and by changes within Protestantism brought about by the rise of the anti-imperialism movement associ-

PRIEST, HEALER, AND DOCTOR

In addition to the many local religious officiants, there are many outstanding healers and priests of international importance in Africa. One of them is Dr. Erick V. A. Gbodossou. He is an ob-gyn and psychiatrist who holds a joint degree in medicine and pharmacy. His experience in traditional medicine goes back to childhood. At the age of two he was chosen to be trained as a healer under the direction of his grandfather and a team of elders. Dr. Gbodossou is now a healer and priest. His spiritual beliefs are based on a saying by Hippocrates: "One cannot be a good physician without being a good priest." He considers this to be the African ancient ideal and one that a traditional healer should not lose sight of. Dr. Gbodossou is the president of PROMETRA International—the Association for the Promotion of Traditional Medicine—in Dakar, Senegal. CEMETRA—Experimental Center for Traditional Medicine—is his medical and research complex; it attracts professionals from all over the world.

ated with the World Council of Churches. Now there is a much greater appreciation of the spirituality of African traditional religion and apologies have been made for past actions and insensitivity.

MEETING NEEDS AND FACING CHALLENGES

In Africa people turn to African religion for their spiritual needs at a variety of levels. Healers, mediums, diviners, rainmakers, priests, elders, rulers, queens, and kings all serve the religious needs of the people. They attain their positions by inheritance or by apprenticeship. In the past they were usually traditional, in the sense that they were not formally educated. Today there are many African religious service providers who hold academic degrees, including PhDs, who serve communities both in Africa and abroad.

However alongside its development and spread, African religion is also subject to many of the problems that affect other religious traditions. For example, the rise of feminism is challenging the male-dominated structures and taboos of much

Members of the Zion Christian Church at an open-air prayer meeting in the streets of Gugulethu, a black township outside Cape Town, South Africa. The Zionist Church is particularly strong in South Africa, with more than 5 million members drawn largely from the Zulu and Swazi people. The church has Protestant mission origins but has blended itself into traditional African culture within a generation. Its practice emphasizes healing and spiritual experience and draws upon elements of traditional African religion.

of African religion. Whether this is to do with female circumcision—now more commonly and controversially called "female genital mutilation"—or the traditional authority given primarily to men, or the abuse of women within traditional notions of female subservience to men, feminism presents as many challenges to African religion as it does to other faiths.

YOUTH CULTURE

The drift of young people away from traditional cultures and models of authority is another problem. The role of the elder is no longer one that can be assumed. The urbanization of much of the African population means that many young people have never known the traditional structures of family, tribe, or village that are the mainstays of African religion. Growing global communications, such as the Internet, offer an influential youth culture that so many young urban Africans desire, and ultimately shrinks or even denies the role of elders and collective ancient wisdom. This is not only breaking the ties that bound people to traditional religion, it is also placing strains on other religious communities such as the Christian churches.

EXPLOITATION OF TRADITIONAL PRACTICES

The lack of clear structures of authority also poses problems for African religion, because it leaves it open to exploitation by people who abuse its power and structures of power. Because of the informal nature of African religion, it is difficult to counter claims by groups that call themselves traditional African religion, even if they seem to be clear aberrations. For example, issues such as the supposed ritual use of bush meat, for which wildlife such as gorillas and chimpanzees are slain, featured in a 2006 trial in the United States, where differing understandings of African tradition were argued in court.

HOLDING ON TO AFRICAN IDENTITY

The rise of a more fundamentalist Islam in some parts of Africa has led to the suppression of many elements of traditional African religion that formerly found a home or at least an umbrella in Islam. Within Christianity the degree to which African traditional religion maintains a distinct identity is increasingly looking doubtful. The same Westernizing influences that turn young people away from tradition are likewise affecting these indigenous churches. Nevertheless it is perhaps within such churches that African religion can best hold on in areas where it is no longer the dominant tradition.

Worldwide, traditional religions are losing ground to other faiths or simply to secularism and Westernization. In 1993 the *State of Religion Atlas* (Simon and Schuster) listed eight African countries in which traditional beliefs were the majority religion. By the 2007 edition this had dropped to five.

Despite some degree of decline in Africa, however, African religion continues to be practiced widely and is finding a place outside Africa. Priests of African religion appear to be in demand for their spiritual service internationally. The popularity of Web sites such as "Outstanding Priests of Traditional African Religion" indicates that the Americas and the United Kingdom are increasingly becoming homes of the religion.

FACT FILE

Worldwide Numbers
Of Africa's population of more than 930 million people, most are influenced by African traditional religion and a significant proportion practice some form of it.

Holy Symbol
The Adinkira symbol is one expression of the supremacy of God in traditional beliefs.

Holy Writings
The religion is based on oral traditions: There are no specific holy writings.

Holy Places
There are no specific pilgrimage sites.

Founders
There is no specific founder of African traditional religion.

Festivals
In Africa, each tribal community has it own celebrations. These are mainly related to coming-of-age, the seasons, and harvests. Kwanzaa is an African-American holiday celebrated annually (December 26–January 1) in the United States to pay tribute to the cultural roots of African Americans.

BIBLIOGRAPHY

Asihene, Emmanuel V. *Traditional Folk-Tales of Ghana*. Lewiston, N.Y.: The Edwin Mellen Press, 1997.

Baker, Sir Samuel White. "The Races of the Nile Basin," in *Transactions of the Ethnological Society of London*, N.S. v (1867), p.231.

Baur, John. *2000 Years of Christianity in Africa: An African Church History*. Nairobi, Kenya: Paulines, 1998.

Bierlein, J.F. *Parallel Myths*. New York: Ballantine Books, 1994.

Boadle, Anthony. "Yoruba Deity Worshipers Open Congress in Havana," in *Havana Journal*. URL: http://havanajournal.com/culture/entry/yoruba_deity_worshipers_open_congress_in_havana. Accessed on February 10, 2009.

Danquah, J. B. *The Akan Doctrine of God: A Fragment of Gold Coast Ethics and Religion*. London: Cass, 1968.

di Nola, A.M., and Patrick O'Connor. *The Prayers of Man*. London: William Heinemann, 1962.

Idowu, E. Bolaji. *Olodumare: God in Yoruba Belief*. London: Longmans, 1966.

Kaigh, Frederick. *Witchcraft and Magic of Africa*. [London]: R. Lesley, 1947.

King, Noel Q. *Religions of Africa*. New York: Harper & Row, 1970.

Lienhardt, G. *Divinity and Experience: The Religion of the Dinka*. Oxford: Clarendon Press, 1961.

Pachocinski, Ryszard. *Proverbs of Africa: Human Nature in the Nigerian Oral Tradition ; an Exposition and Analysis of 2,600 Proverbs from 64 Peoples*. St. Paul, Minn.: Professors World Peace Academy, 1996.

Parrinder, Geoffrey. *African Traditional Religion*. New York: Harper & Row, 1962.

Potter, Paul. *Hippocrates, Volume VIII*. Cambridge, Mass.: Harvard University Press, 1995.

Rattray, R. S. *Religion & Art in Ashanti*. New York: AMS Press, 1979.

Richardson, John. *A Life of Picasso*. New York: Random House, 1991.

Roscoe, John. *The Baganda: An Account of Their Native Customs and Beliefs*. London: Macmillan & Co. Ltd., 1911.

Segy, Ladislas. *African Sculpture Speaks*. New York: Da Capo Press, 1975.

Sproul, Barbara. *Primal Myths: Creation Myths Around the World*. San Francisco: Harper San Francisco, 1991.

Vatican Council, and Walter M. Abbott. *The Documents of Vatican II*. New York: Guild Press, 1966.

Welbourn, Frederick Burkewood. *Religion and Politics in Uganda, 1952–1962*. Nairobi: East African Pub. House, 1965.

FURTHER READING

Achebe, Chinua. *Things Fall Apart.* New York: Doubleday and Company, 1994.

Bellegarde-Smith, Patrick. *Fragments of Bone: Neo-African Religions in a New World.* Urbana: University of Illinois Press, 2005.

Bohannan, Paul. *Africa and Africans,* 4th ed. Prospect Heights, Ill.: Waveland Press, 1999.

Breuilly, Elizabeth, Joanne O'Brien, Martin Palmer, and Martin E. Marty. *Religions of the World: The Illustrated Guide to Origins, Beliefs, Traditions & Festivals.* New York: Checkmark Books, 2005.

Brodd, Jeffrey. *World Religions: A Voyage of Discovery.* Winona, Minn.: Saint Mary's Press, 2003.

Clarke, Peter B. *New Trends and Developments in African Religions.* Conn.: Greenwood Press, 1998.

Fisher, Robert B. *West African Religions Traditions: Focus on the Akan of Ghana.* New York: Orbis Books, 1998.

Isichei, Elizabeth. *A History of Christianity in Africa.* Grand Rapids, Mich.: Wm. B. Eerdmans Publishing Co., 1995.

Kinsley, David R. *Health, Healing and Religion: A Cross Cultural Perspective.* Upper Saddle River, N.J.: Prentice Hall, 1995.

Lawson, E. Thomas. *Religions of Africa: Traditions in Transformation,* 2nd ed. Prospect Heights, Ill.: Waveland Press, 1998.

Lewis-Williams, J. David. *A Cosmos In Stone: Interpreting Religion and Society Through Rock Art.* Walnut Creek, Calif.: AltaMira Press, 2002.

Magesa, Laurenti. *African Religion: The Moral Traditions of Abundant Life.* New York: Orbis Books, 1997.

Mbiti, John S. *African Religions & Philosophy.* Portsmouth, N.H.: Heinemann, 1992.

Murphy, Larry. *Down by the Riverside: Readings in African American Religion.* New York: New York University Press, 2000.

O'Brien, Joanne, Martin Palmer, David B. Barrett, and Joanne O'Brien. *The Atlas of Religion.* Berkeley, Calif.: University of California Press, 2007.

Ray, Benjamin C. *African Religions: Symbol, Ritual, and Community*, 2nd ed. Cambridge, U.K.: Pearson Education, 1999.

Some, Malidoma Patrice. *The Healing Wisdom of Africa: Finding Life Purpose Through Nature, Ritual, and Community.* New York: Penguin Putnam Inc., 1998.

Tutu, Desmond, ed. *The African Prayer Book.* New York: Doubleday and Company, 1995.

WEB SITES

Further facts and figures, history, and current status of the religion can be found on the following Web sites:

www.afrikaworld.net/afrel
A major source of information on African Traditional Religion. Provides topical information and an insight into the relationships with Christianity and Islam.

www.sacred-texts.com/afr/index.htm
An electronic version of rare public-domain books about African traditional religion.

www.africa.upenn.edu/About_African/ww_relig.html
A broad-based resource on African traditional religion from the University of Pennsylvania's African Studies Center.

www.nationmaster.com/encyclopedia/African-traditional-religion
An outline of the faith.

GLOSSARY

Aksum or Axum—The name of a capital and of an ancient kingdom of Ethiopia.

ancestors—Forebears whose distinguished position in a community qualify their spirits to be regarded with veneration.

associates of the Supreme Being—In African religion these are the deities, divinities, or gods holding spiritual power that is subordinated to the power of the Supreme Being.

Candomblé—A Brazilian version of Yoruba religion.

Chukwu—The name by which the Igbo people of Nigeria call God. It means the "Great Spirit." Copts—Indigenous Egyptians.

cubism—A style of painting and sculpture noted for the reduction of natural forms to geometric ones, which, to a certain extent, was influenced by African art.

Da—The Fon divinity of the cult of the serpent.

divination—The art of interpreting human events and situations, discovering the past, revealing future events, and obtaining any required information by using specified techniques.

diviner—A ritual leader who is qualified to conduct the art of divination.

duality—A term applied to the African concept of the Supreme Being, in which the Supreme Being is understood to be one but in two constituents.

Ebasi—The name of the Supreme Being for the Duala people of Cameroon. It means "the Omnipotent Father."

Esu—The divinity in the Yoruba pantheon of gods who is charged with the office of inspector general in the theocratic government of the Supreme Being.

ethnic group—A community or a people that shares a common distinctive culture, religion, language, and other connecting links. In an African context the term is preferred as a substitute for the colonially loaded and misused word tribe.

extrahuman forces—Mystical forces that include magic, witchcraft, and sorcery.

Fa—The Fon divinity of divination.

Falasha—A member of the African Ethiopian Jewish community.

Fon—A people of Benin, formerly known as Dahomey, whose religion on the basis of its concept of Vodun has had a noticeable influence in the Western Hemisphere.

Ggulu—The divinity of the sky in the Baganda pantheon of gods.

guardian spirit—A spirit identified as watching over the interests of a group of people, such as an extended family, a clan, or an ethnic group. Such spirits are symbolized by mountains, extraordinary trees, rocks, waterfalls, animals, reptiles, and so on.

healer—A ritual leader who is endowed with the knowledge of herbal medicine by superhuman powers, inheritance, and training. He or she may be referred to as a medicine man or woman, an herbalist, or many other familiar names in local languages.

herbalist—A person who conducts healing practices with superhuman assistance, mainly by using herbal medicine.

heroes—Legendary people whose feats in a community have distinguished them, sometimes to the extent of being made into gods.

Imana—The primary name used by the Banyarwanda and Barundi of Central Africa to express their concept of the Supreme Being.

iNkosi yeZulu—In the language of the Zulu people of South Africa, "the Lord of the sky or heaven."

Jakuta—The divinity and functionary of the Supreme Being's ministry of justice in the Yoruba pantheon of gods.

kaffir—A term of abuse from Islam used to describe a person who has no faith; an infidel, unbeliever.

Kaffraria—A land of unbelievers.

Katonda—The name by which the Baganda of Uganda call the Supreme Being. It means "Creator," "Originator."

Kazooba—The name for God used by some African peoples, such as the Bazinza of Tanzania, Banyankore, and the Baganda of Uganda. The name means "the Sun," which is used here metaphorically to mean the Supreme Being.

Kibuuka—The divinity of war in the Baganda pantheon of gods.

Kiwanuka—The divinity of thunder, lightning, and fertility in the Baganda pantheon of gods.

Kwanzaa—The holiday based on the African first-fruits celebrations, intended to pay tribute to the rich cultural roots of African Americans.

Kwoth—The name used by the Nuer of Sudan to express their concept of the Supreme Being. It means "spirit."

Kyala—The name for the Supreme Being among the Nyakyusa of Tanzania. It means "Owner of all things."

Legba—The divine trickster in the Fon religion. Legba determines the fortunes and misfortunes of people; he is the messenger between the Supreme Being and other gods.

Leve—The name for the Supreme Being among the Mende of Sierra Leone.

Leza—The primary name used by the Ambo and Baila of Zambia to express their concept of the Supreme Being. It means "Creator."

Lubaale—The pantheon of the Baganda religion of Uganda. Katonda, the Baganda name for the Supreme Being, is not strictly part of Lubaale. He is above Lubaale as the Creator and metaphorical father of the Balubaale, the plural form of Lubaale.

Mabee—The name by which the Bulu people of Cameroon call the Supreme Being. It means "the One who bears the world."

Macumba—A Brazilian version of the Yoruba religion.

magic—The ability and practice of manipulating mysterious forces for practical ends.

mangu—An innate substance in a person's body that is believed to carry the germ of witchcraft.

Mawu-Lisa—The hyphenated divinity that makes up the Fon pantheon of the sky gods. Mawu is female and Lisa is male; together they advance the work of creation initiated by Nana-Buluku.

medium—A person who is capable of being possessed by a spirit.

mhondoro—Spirits that were associated with the ruling dynasties of Great Zimbabwe.

Modimo—The name for the Supreme Being among the Tswana people of Botswana in Southern Africa. It means "Greatest Ancestral Spirit."

monotheism—A system of a belief in one God.

Mukasa—The divinity of fertility, health, wealth, and general welfare in the Baganda pantheon of gods.

Mulungu—The name for the Supreme Being among the Gogo ethnic group of Tanzania and the Chewa ethnic group of Malawi.

Musisi—The divinity in charge of earthquakes in the Baganda pantheon of gods.

Musoke—The rainbow spirit in the Baganda pantheon of gods.

Mvelamqandi—The name for the Supreme Being among the Swazi people of Swaziland. It means "the One who appears first."

Mwari—The name of the Supreme Being among the Shona people of Zimbabwe.

Nana-Buluku—The name used by the Fon people of Benin to express the idea of the Supreme Being as the Creator.

Ngai—The name for God used by the Kikuyu and Akamba ethnic groups of Kenya. It is also used by the Masai, who live both in Kenya and Tanzania. The name means "the Creator, the Divider, the Benefactor, the Possessor of Brightness."

Nyambi—The name for the Supreme Being and Creator of everything among the Barotse people of Zambia. Their concept of the Supreme Being is distinguished by their belief that Nyambi had a wife, whose name is Nasilele.

Nyame—The name for the Supreme Being among the Ashanti of Ghana. It means "Shining One."

Nzambi—The name by which the Vili people of the Congo know the Supreme Being. It means "Creator and Ultimate Source of Power."

Ogun—The divinity of war and iron in the Yoruba pantheon of gods; patron of all works connected with iron, and presiding divinity over matters concerned with oaths, covenants, and pacts.

Olodumare—The name for the Supreme Being among the Yoruba people. It means "Most Supreme Being."

Onyankopon—The name for the Supreme Being among the Akan people of Ivory Coast and Ghana. It means "Alone the Great One."

Orisa—The pantheon of the Yoruba religion.

Orisanla—Second in command in the Yoruba pantheon of gods. Also known as Obatala, this divinity holds the position of associate creator.

Orunmilla—The divinity of divination in the Yoruba pantheon of gods.

pantheon—In the context of African religion, all national gods collectively considered.

phansi—The habitation place of spirits, believed by the Zulu to be below the surface of the Earth.

polytheism—Belief in a hierarchy of many gods.

priest—The overseer, administrator, and coordinator of matters that relate to divine premises, such as temple of a god. The priest officiates over the rites pertaining to the temple and sacred grounds.

rainmaker—A person capable of effectively praying for the rain to fall and for it to stop.

rites—Ceremonial, customary, and prescribed practices that punctuate all aspects of life in African religion.

rites of passage—The ceremonies, customs, and practices that are performed in order to religiously enable people to move smoothly through turning points of their lives, from their earliest to their last moment of existence on Earth.

ritual—The actualization of a belief system; a ceremonial act.

Rog—The name for the Supreme Being among the Serer of Gambia and Senegal. It means "Creator."

Ruhanga—The name by which the Banyankore and Banyoro of Uganda know the Supreme Being. It means "Creator and Fixer of everything."

Ruwa—The name by which the Chagga of Tanzania know the Supreme Being. It means "the Sun."

Sagbata—The Fon divinity of the Earth.

Sango—Like Jakuta, a Yoruba divinity and functionary in God's ministry of justice.

Se—The Fon divinity of the souls of human beings.

Sogbo—The Fon divinity of thunder and the sea.

sorcery—Wicked magic intended to hurt others.

spirit—A bodiless and superhuman power, force, or vital element, which human beings are mindful of with reverence.

spirit world—Spirits collectively considered.

spirits of the departed—The souls of particular human beings and other animated creatures, which are transformed into spirits at the moment when they are separated from the body, and which are regarded with reverence.

spiritual guardian—A spirit identified as watching over the interests of a group of people.

Suku—The name for the Supreme Being among the Ovimbundu of Angola. It means "He who supplies the needs of His creatures."

superhuman beings—Gods, ancestors, guardian spirits, and spirits of the departed, who are regarded as powers above human beings.

Supreme Being—the unique power above which there is no other.

taboo—A prohibition from doing something or using something because of its reverential nature.

ubuntu—Being truly human.

Uluhlanga—The name for the Supreme Being used by the Ngoni people of Malawi. It means "the Original Source."

unity—A term applied to the ideas and concept of the Supreme Being to reflect the Supreme Being as one and uniquely one.

Unkulunkulu—The name for the Supreme Being used by the Zulu of South Africa and the Ndebele of Zimbabwe. It means "the Great Oldest One."

Vidye—The name by which the Baluba of Congo know the Supreme Being. It means "Great Creator Spirit."

vital force—The invisible power that is believed to underlie and energize a variety of objects of the Supreme Being's creation.

Vodun—The Fon pantheon of gods.

Walumbe—The divinity of death in the Baganda pantheon of gods.

Wanga—The divinity charged with fixing what goes wrong in the Baganda pantheon of gods.

Wene—The name for the Supreme Being among the Tallensi of Burkina Faso. It means "sky god."

witch—A person who has in himself or herself an innate power or force of witchcraft.

witchcraft—A cause of misfortune in a community.

Yala—The name for the Supreme Being among the Kpelle of Liberia.

Yataa—The name for the Supreme Being among the Kono people of Sierra Leone. It means "the One you meet everywhere."

Zambi—The name by which the Baya of the Central African Republic know the Supreme Being. It means "Creator."

zulu—The sky or heaven.

INDEX

A

Abaluyia people of Kenya:
    sacrifices 76
Africa: the arts 13, 111–112,
    120–121; culture 106;
    European explorers
    24–25, 122–123; geog-
    raphy of 91, 118–122;
    history of 13–15, 18–20,
    116–125; independence
    106, 114, 125–128;
    Kwanzaa 108; mission-
    aries in 24–25; modern
    Africa 128–131; music
    75, 109–110; the oral
    tradition 16, 26–35; slave
    trade in 24; spread of
    religion in 10–13, 15–18,
    20–25, 112
African Sculpture Speaks (Segy)
    95, 100, 112
AIDS virus 72
Akamba people of Kenya:
    Mumbi (god) 44
Akan people of Ivory Coast:
    Ananse, the spider 33; art
    36; god as the origina-
    tor 40; Nyame (god) 35;
    Onyankopan (god) 44;
    proverbs 35
Alur people of Uganda: Jok
    (god) 44
Ambo people of Zambia:
    Leza (god) 43
Angola: Bacongo people of
    45; Ovimbundu people
    of 41, 45
animals, as spirits 49, 90
arts, the 13, 111–112,
    120–121

Ashanti people of Ghana 40;
    Nyame (god) 44; puberty
    rites 69
Azande people of Sudan:
    magic and witchcraft 98,
    101

B

Baamba people: priests 83
Bacongo people of Angola:
    Nzambi (god) 45
Baganda people of Uganda
    42; birth and 66–68;
    Ggulu (god) 58–59;
    Katonda (god) 44;
    Kibuuka (god) 60, 125;
    Kitaka (god) 59; Kiwa-
    nuka (god) 59; Lubaale
    Mukasa 30–32, 58–60;
    proverb 41; Mukasa
    (god) 30, 33, 60; Musisi
    (god) 60; return of relics
    125; Walumbe (god) 59;
    Wanga (god) 59–60
Baila people of Zambia 40;
    Leza (god) 43
Bakiga people 41
Baluba people of Congo:
    Vidye (god) 43
Bambara people of West
    Africa: Bemba or Ngala
    (god) 39
Bambuti people of Congo 40
Bamum people of Camer-
    oon: Njinyi (god) 43
Banyankore people of
    Uganda 40; priests 83;
    Ruhanga (god) 44
Banyarwanda people of
    Rwanda: conception

and creation 66; and 40;
    Imana (god) 43
Barotse people of Zambia:
    Nyambi (god) 43
Barundi people of Central
    Africa 42; conception
    and creation 66; Imana
    (god) 43; and magic 101
Basuto people of Lesotho:
    Molimo (god) 45
Bavenda people of South
    Africa: priests 83
Baya people of Central
    Africa: Zambi (god) 43
Bazinza people of Tanzania:
    Kazooba (god) 44
Bemba (god) 39
Bemba people of Central
    Africa: and magic 98
Benin 12; Fon people of 39,
    44, 60–63
Binawa people of Nigeria:
    priests 83
birth, rituals for 66–69
Black Jews 18–20
Botswana 12; Tswana people
    of 45
bride payment (*lobola*) 72
Bulu people of Cameroon:
    Mabee (god) 43
burial 50, 74
Burkina Faso 12; Tallensi
    people of 44

C

Cameroon: Bamum people
    of 43; Bulu people of 43;
    Duala people of 43
Chagga people of Tanzania:
    Ruwa (god) 44

75; objects for 18, 95; prayers 10, 16, 50, 69, 74–75, 103; rainmakers 85–87; ritual leaders 79–85; sacred spaces 88–95; sacrifices 16, 54, 63, 76, 91; spirits and 48

Rog (god) 44, 45

Ruhanga (god) 44

Ruwa (god) 44

Rwanda, Banyarwanda people of 40, 43, 66

S

sacred space 88–95

sacrifices 16, 54, 63, 76, 91

Sagbata (god) 61

Sango (god) 58

San people of southern Africa 121

Se (god) 61–63

sculptures 121–122; as ritual objects 95

Segy, Ladislas 95, 100, 112

Serer people 44, 45

Shilluk people of Sudan: Juok (god) 44

Shona people of Zimbabwe: Mwari (god) 45, 93

shrines 16, 91–93, 94

Sierra Leone 12; Kono people of 45; Mende people of 45

slave trade, the 24

Sonjo people of Tanzania: priests 83

sorcery 101–103

spirits 46–63; animal spirits 49, 90

spiritual suffering 15

Srubu people of Nigeria: priests 83

Sudan: Azande people of 98; Dinka people of 30, 44, 87; Nuer people of 42, 44; Shilluk people of 44

Suku (god) 45

Sun, the 90, 91

Supreme Being 35, 46–47; attributes of 39; monotheism 36–37; nature of 38–39; originator of the universe 29–30, 40; the possessor 42; prayers to 75; the provider 41; sacrifices to 66, 76, 91 *see also* god (names for)

Swazi people of Swaziland: Mvelamqandi (god) 45

T

taboos, during pregnancy 68

Tallensi people of Burkina Faso: Wene (god) 44

Tanzania: Bazinza people of 44; Chagga people of 44; Gogo people of 44; Nyakyusa people of 44, 101; Sonjo people of 83

temples and tombs 93, 94

Tswana people of Botswana: Modimo (god) 45

Tunisia 13; Christianity in 20

U

Uganda: Alur people of 44; Baganda people of 30–32, 41, 42, 44, 58–60, 66–68, 125; Banyankore people of 40, 44, 83; Kabakas people of 94; Langi people of 98

Uluhlanga (god) 45

United States, African religions in 109, 111, 114

Unkulunkulu (god) 45

V

Vidye (god) 43

Vili people of Congo: Nzambi (god) 43

W

Walumbe (god) 59

Wanga (god) 59–60

weddings 71–72

Wene (god) 44

witch doctors 85, 100, 115

witchcraft 98–101, 103

women: female circumcision 69, 130; feminism and 128–130

Y

Yataa (god) 45

Yoruba people of Nigeria: diviners 82; Esu (god) 54–57; Jakuta 58; Ogun (god) 57; Olodumare (god) 30, 45; Orisana 53–54; Orunmilla 53, 54; the Orisa 53–58; proverb 8; sculptures 121–122; Sango (god) 58; shrine of Ogun 94

Z

Zambi (god) 43

Zambia: Ambo people of 43; Baila people of 40, 43; Barotse people of 43

Zimbabwe: "Great Zimbabwe" 92; Ndebele people of 45; Shona people of 45, 93

Zulu people of Southern Africa 40; marriage 71, 72; origination 90; Unkulunkulu (god) 45

ABOUT THE AUTHOR

Aloysius M. Lugira is adjunct associate professor of theology and religion at Boston College in Chestnut Hill, Massachusetts. He has authored numerous books and articles on African religion.

ABOUT THE SERIES EDITORS

Martin Palmer is the founder of ICOREC (International Consultancy on Religion, Education, and Culture) in 1983 and is the secretary-general of the Alliance of Religions and Conservation (ARC). He is the author of many books on world religions.

Joanne O'Brien has an M.A. degree in theology and has written a range of educational and general reference books on religion and contemporary culture. She is co-author, with Martin Palmer and Elizabeth Breuilly, of *Religions of the World* and *Festivals of the World* published by Facts On File Inc.

PICTURE CREDITS